Psychology Revivals

The Beloved Ego

Wilhelm Stekel was an Austrian physician and psychologist and one of Freud's earliest followers. A prolific writer, this book originally published in 1921, was considered by the translator 'the best general introduction of its author to the English public', containing as is does many of his central ideas. Although the author had already fallen out with him by this time, in the preface to this book, he acknowledges Freud's significance to the field and says he regards his 'Psycho-Analysis as being a step towards a new psycho-therapy'.

The Beloved Ego

Foundations of the new study of the psyche

Wilhelm Stekel

Routledge
Taylor & Francis Group
LONDON AND NEW YORK

First published in 1921
by Kegan Paul, Trench, Trubner & Co., Ltd

This edition first published in 2014 by Routledge
27 Church Road, Hove BN3 2FA

and by Routledge
711 Third Avenue, New York, NY 10017

Routledge is an imprint of the Taylor & Francis Group, an informa business

Publisher's Note
The publisher has gone to great lengths to ensure the quality of this reprint but points out that some imperfections in the original copies may be apparent.

Disclaimer
The publisher has made every effort to trace copyright holders and welcomes correspondence from those they have been unable to contact.

A Library of Congress record exists under LC control no.: 22005823

ISBN: 978-1-138-01841-9 (hbk)
ISBN: 978-1-315-77965-2 (ebk)

THE BELOVED EGO

FOUNDATIONS OF THE NEW STUDY OF
THE PSYCHE

BY

WILHELM STEKEL, M.D.

Neurologist and Psycho-therapist, Vienna

AUTHORIZED TRANSLATION

BY

ROSALIE GABLER

Member of the British Psychological Society, and of the Society for the Study of Orthopsychics

LONDON

KEGAN PAUL, TRENCH, TRUBNER & CO., LTD.

NEW YORK: MOFFAT YARD & COMPANY

1921

MADE IN GREAT BRITAIN.

DR. STEKEL'S PREFACE TO THE ENGLISH EDITION

My first attempt at an English preface. To begin with: I am happy to wear an English dress! I have been longing for many years to speak to English readers. I feel very thankful. Few men are thankful. . . . I am proud to say I have conquered the two most mean of human qualities, envy, and ingratitude. I have overcome both the envy of ingratitude and the ingratitude of envy.

To continue: One of my first and best teachers in Psychology was an Englishman, whom Swinburne, my beloved Swinburne, the creator of "The Ballad of Dreamland" addresses: "Not if men's tongues and angels' all in one spake, might the word be said that might speak Thee. All stars are angels; but the sun is God."

In case all of my future readers may not have been readers of Swinburne, I will give this teacher's name: Shakespeare, now in the Heaven of Immortals.

You can find in his works all the riddles of the beloved Ego. You can find there the unspoken, the unforeseen, the only guessed, the only foreboded, the secret mysteries of human Unconsciousness. He knows the depths and the heights, the brilliant light and the darkening shadow, the virtues and what lies behind them, the hidden crimes and their concealed origins.

If it be true that every genius of a nation (like

every criminal!) represents the collective soul of his people, every English reader is a little Shakespeare. I hope they are only very little Shakespeares and so will not be too severe with his humble Austrian pupil.

I know that many English readers will laugh at my mistakes and at my German English. But I hope they will also feel the warmth of my heart for their culture, and will understand I am striving to comprehend my beloved authors in their own language.

Translations are very rarely new creations! Every translated book is like a masked lady, clothed in a strange dress for a masquerade. I am afraid they may either over-value the worth and the beauty of the true face—or they may think the nice costume covers an ugly figure beneath.

But I hope one thing will remain unchanged and undestroyable: the truth of eternal thoughts, the power of healing knowledge and, last but not least, my warm love for mankind and my pity for the sufferings and writhings of tortured and oppressed souls.

WILHELM STEKEL.

VIENNA.

AUTHOR'S PREFACE

IT has taken a long time to realize that the so-called nervous diseases are diseases of the Psyche. Now a great change is taking place. Most nerve-specialists are becoming doctors of the soul. They interest themselves in the experiences and the *milieu* of the patient; they investigate his attitude towards the world; they correct his wrong views; and they try to draw him away from the harmful twilight of his fantasies and bring him into harmony with reality. The doctor has become educator, father-confessor, and teacher of humanity.

To have been one of the first to foresee and investigate these connecting links is my humble merit. I began as a "wild" explorer of the Psyche till I met with the much-discussed teachings of Freud, which opened up a new world to me. Freud called his method of investigating the soul "Psycho-Analysis." He attaches the greatest importance to the discovery of the deeply buried childish impressions of a sexual nature. The exposure of these repressions should bring with it healing.

I have retained the best of this teaching, and from it have evolved a new one.

This does not indicate that I wish to minimize the pioneer work of the great Viennese master. On the shoulders of a giant, even a dwarf can see farther than the giant can; and eventually it is the fate of every pupil to outstrip the master if he wishes to become master himself.

Thus I regard Freud's Psycho-Analysis as being a step towards a new psycho-therapy. To glance into the past is necessary. The doctor must analyze his patient if he wants to help him. But not according to pre-conceived opinions and definite schemes. The danger of every science is routine. Every new soul must mean a new problem for the soul-investigator.

People erroneously believe—as can be seen from the way in which opponents treat the matter—that Psycho-Analysis consists of a painful inquiry into sexual experiences. The real analyst does not inquire, he takes the confessions to himself, and is well on his guard against showing the patient by suggestive questions some path of soul-investigation which might easily prove misleading. We certainly do not wish to undervalue the importance of sexuality in the psychic life of civilized man. But we must also guard ourselves against over-estimation. Sexuality is only *one* of the questions which are of importance; and this little book will show that there are also many others. The treatment aims at the reconciliation of the patient with reality, showing to him those of his fantasies which are incapable of fulfilment, and indicating the necessary re-adjustment of his morbid attitude towards his immediate surroundings and towards the whole world. Every neurotic lives in a second world of his own. Into this world the doctor of the soul has to penetrate. It holds all his past, it builds up his present and directs his aims into the future, far beyond human powers.

After recognition and understanding, there

follow teaching and expansion, leading and guiding.

The doctor must also become the educator of the patient.

Analysis, which is really only a disintegrating, destructive process, must be followed by a recombining and reconstructive building process.

Analysis dismantles the old fortress-walls, the gloomy strongholds, the dilapidated ruins of neurosis. These must be replaced by new, habitable, and cheerful edifices built up by the soul. The doctor must give his patient an aim and purpose in life, and a practicable outlook in life.

In the following sketches I have drawn some small studies, which will bear witness to my endeavour to fulfil this difficult task. They contain much analytical material, and also the substance of a synthesis of a new and sounder conception of life.

I hope they will be of use to teach the healthy, and to set free the sick. As a whole they show clearly the difficulties of the calling of a doctor of the soul. Intricate, obscure problems from a bizarre, almost caricatured world of fantasy press themselves upon him, demanding solution. How would this be possible, unless the thinker, the poet, and the physician were united in one? Unless the whole of his powers were made use of in the high calling of a priest and leader? This little book deals with all these questions by giving the first outlines of many problems with which the author is dealing more extensively in larger scientific works. It contains foundations for a new dietetic of the soul. I have used the title

Grundzüge * because on this I intend to build, out of the conclusions I have arrived at from my own experience. These essays are in an artistic form. I have always aimed at presenting my thoughts in an attractive style, avoiding the dry form of the man of science. The time is past when it was considered inevitable that scientific language should produce boredom. It is a generally accepted fact that a doctor must be an artist; how much more so should this be the case with a doctor of souls.

It is not every doctor who is suitable for this difficult vocation; and therefore different results are obtained by the different methods of different doctors. *For it is the doctor who heals, and not the method.*

WILHELM STEKEL.

VIENNA, *April, 1913.*

* The German title of the book is *Das Liebe Ich: Grundzüge einer neuen Dietätik der Seele.*

TRANSLATOR'S PREFACE

Clothed in popular form "The Beloved Ego," by Dr. W. Stekel, will serve as the best general introduction of its author to the English public. The quantity and literary interest of the works of this distinguished Viennese Psychotherapist, teacher and writer, have made him well known throughout the continents of Europe and America. It is time for the English public to have an opportunity to appreciate the value of Dr. Stekel's work.

The present book, though so simple and delightful in form, nevertheless contains some of the central ideas of the author—ideas which have been developed and worked out at great length, and with great skill, in a long series of learned and technical volumes.

Stekel presents to us a clear, if slightly disillusioned, view of life. Yet one which is wholesome and brave, laying special stress on the necessity for joy in life.

In all this he is a physician of the soul. But he is also a poet, and this in no figurative sense. He has published a volume of poems full of insight, and he has also written plays which clothe in living form his experiences as a thinker in contact with the minds and lives of his patients. All his writings show exceptional literary skill and first-hand knowledge of the great World Literature. Yet, with all this culture, Stekel is very much himself—an independent and individual mind.

In translating I have endeavoured to retain as

far as possible the author's individual style and grace in the original. But it must necessarily lose much in translation owing to the impossibility of transcribing the intimate idiom of the original into a foreign language.

In conclusion I wish to tender my grateful thanks to my co-worker, H. Coxeter, and to those of my friends who have so willingly and generously helped me in my task.

ROSALIE GABLER.

CONTENTS

THE BELOVED EGO

CHAPTER I

THE BELOVED EGO

THERE is an old fairy story, full of deep meaning, which tells of a king who so detested vanity that he declared that he would only give his daughter in marriage to the man who could be proved to be the least vain, and that he only should inherit his kingdom. For this end he put up a large looking-glass, and watched the people passing by it. Every one looked into the alluring glass, and especially the suitors, to reassure themselves for the last time as to the impression they would create. The old king had just begun to give up all hope of the success of this test, when a plain-looking man came along deep in thought. He passed the looking-glass without noticing it; and was greatly surprised when he was led in triumph to the king. The lucky man was a poet, and had just been thinking about one of his poems. Thus he had gained the king's daughter and throne through his silent song.

So much for the fairy tale.

The kings in fairy tales generally have a better knowledge of human nature than this. Our poet had not even seen the looking-glass. Perhaps if he had noticed it, he would not have passed it so carelessly. Even if he had noticed the glass and yet passed it by, he might still have been the vainest of the vain, because he saw himself reflected meanwhile in the mirror of his soul—vanity such as this is much worse than the former, which over-estimates the outer man. If one has had the opportunity of knowing an artist—not as he pretends to be, but as he really is—one will always be astonished at the immense amount of vanity he produces for the admiration of his Ego. Is not all his creation the result of a vanity which tries to force his Ego on his fellow beings? Where shall one find a poet who writes only for himself, and ignores recognition and fame when the certainty of its attainment is assured?

So-called vanity disappears without a mirror to reflect it. We adorn ourselves for others, but only that others may help to increase our own self-estimation. Vanity needs a sounding-board in order to emphasize it.

Vanity is but the expression of self-love, and self-love always craves for the approbation and appreciation of one's fellows. We want to be admired by others, but only so as to be able to admire ourselves the more.

What a splendid word was the commandment "Love thy neighbour as thyself!" What mortal could ever rise to this god-like height without self-deception?

No human being has any perception of the immense power of self-love, nor can he have it, because his judgement is clouded by the affect; and yet just because this quality hides itself so modestly from the world and from the Ego, we all love ourselves more than we guess: yes, even more!—"We are all in love with ourselves."

An old myth tells us how Narcissus saw his own image reflected in the water, and was thereupon seized with a strong passion for himself. Modern psychiatrists describe extreme degrees of self-love as Narcissism. A continuous line of development stretches from the normal to the pathological, and it is difficult to decide where the normal ends and the pathological begins.

We are all Narcissists; our Ego is to us the centre of the world, and everything by which we are surrounded is only of importance to us in so far as it is illuminated by our Ego-rays. The first period of our life is obviously a time of boundless self-love. The child is absolutely egoistic, and loves only those persons who are at his command. He is gradually educated in love; from Egoism to Altruism! The little egoist is told that he must love this person and that, because they are good to him, and so on. At this period the child feels himself the centre of the universe.

His fantasies conquer for him immense kingdoms in which he is always the ruler, and they create for him boundless possibilities. This over-estimation of the Ego is tremendously increased by the blind admiration of the parents. The child is told a thousand times how beautiful, how dear, how sweet, how enchanting, how lovely he is—and is compelled to believe it, as he is taught to accept the parents' decree. There is a greater danger in this form of education than the educationalist foresees, as the child mind is thus always focussed on an over-estimation of his own Ego, and easily breaks down when hard necessity dissolves the fantastic pictures, and changes the Kingdom of Youth into thraldom of life (a main cause of child suicide). This also accounts for the differences in Narcissism, and why one human being has a greater tendency towards it than another. And even those who may not be openly Narcissistic, certainly pay due tribute to their secret god, i.e., to their Ego (themselves). All phenomena of life present themselves thus in a different aspect. The outer world is only a projection of our inner self, for we only perceive what our Ego-rays can touch.

Perhaps a few definite examples can better explain the phenomenon of Narcissism. Let us begin with that which has called forth the gravest objection against our teaching: with love! Is it not true then that one falls in love with another being so passionately that one may even throw away one's own life if one cannot reach the object of this love?

Where is there self-love in this? Where Egoism?

It is well worth while to study the condition of such a love.

We come to know a person and we are enthusiastic because that person holds the same views as we ourselves. We "suit" each other, which means, in other words, we have found ourselves in him. In the same way we like a play in the theatre if it meets "our" views, a picture when seen with "our" eyes, a poem, when it gives expression to "our" mood. And that girl pleases us who has our own traits. One is often surprised that older married couples look so much alike, and one talks of adaptation, influence of the environment and the results of continually seeing each other. But why does one blind oneself to the fact that lovers very often show a certain likeness to one another? I believe also that love at first sight is only self-love. We see a being who is as we would wish to be ourselves. The poet expresses it thus:

> Was ist dein und was ist mein?—
> Ach, du weisst es nicht,—
> Wie aus *dir* in Lust und Pein—
> *Meine* Seele spricht.

> What is thine? or what is mine?
> Nor in grief or mirth
> Do'st thou know each word of thine
> In my heart had birth?
>
> Translated by B. T. Wyatt Smith.

From of old the power which makes two people love each other is that of self-love. Let us imagine we want to make Max and Anne fall in love with each other. First we tell her how the enchanted Max talked about her; what an impression she made on the young man—that he is quite off his head. We tell Max the same sort of thing; she thought him the nicest of all, and what taking ways he possessed! When next they meet they will both endeavour to show their best side, and in a short time there will spring up a flaming passion. The driving force in this case was the Ego-rays. Self-love, at the appreciation of the other, kindles to a burning glow. The Narcissistic powers stir up powerful emotions into action—and love is projected towards that object which occupies itself with the admiration of the Ego. The loved object is gilded over by the Ego-rays, which were sent out only to return the more resplendent.

Thus we can also understand how people can sit for hours in front of the looking-glass and gaze at their reflection. They are their own lovers and can never get their fill of looking at themselves. They also have a strong inclination to be photographed or painted; they want to see themselves in different positions and costumes. And others again are like the poet in the fairy tale; in their vanity they reflect themselves in the mirror of their own soul. They observe and ponder over themselves, and know only one interest; their own Ego. These are the people who can never truly find themselves; they are searching for some one who will understand them completely and can feel as they do. Where can they find this human being? Every new acquaintance is a fresh disappointment.

The Don Juan also is really only seeking himself, and each new conquest confirms his belief in his own irresistibility. This is a belief which many people possess, and it leads them to behave in a strange manner. Whoever wants to see such individuals need only go to the seaside, to an open-air bath, or in Vienna to the Gaensehaeufel, and he will find people who are only really happy when they can show themselves for hours to their fellow-men and women. Indeed the beloved sun has much to be responsible for; but how many of these very popular sun baths are baths of self-love—and would never be taken at all if the bathers were isolated from each other?

As it is here only a harmless outlet of the impulses, we can regard this with equanimity. But matters become serious when over-estimation leads to reckless actions and brings people into conflict with the law. The newspapers described recently a scene in Venice, which they called "Eve before the Judges." The accused (a peasant woman) suddenly flung off all her clothes without apparent motive, and stood naked before the judges; who condemned her for this to a heavy sentence of imprisonment. This simple peasant woman still had a dim memory from ancient times, when the belief in the enchanting power of the body led to strange customs. There were forms of bewitchment in which one was compelled to undress, and there is also the legend of the beautiful witch-devil who appeared before the solitary hermit in dazzling nakedness.

This boundless over-estimation of the Ego has another unfortunate aspect. Through the disappointments of life or other physical causes, it changes into its opposite; because all life appears in a double form (the law of bi-polarity). If the Ego-rays can magnify their own Ego and minimize the surroundings, they are also capable of magnifying the surroundings and minimizing the Ego. Such people suffer from a pathological modesty and shyness. They have a torturing sense of their own inferiority. They do not trust themselves with any difficult task. They cannot command. They are only happy if others care, work, organize for, and command them, and without support they are feeble, waving reeds in the wind. It is incredible to them that they can please others.

Ich kann es nicht fassen, nicht glauben,—
Es hat ein Traum mich berückt,—
Wie hätt'er doch unter allen—
Mich Arme erhöht und begluckt.

I cannot, dare not believe it,
A dreamy sense has beguil'd,—
How could he from all our maidens
Choose me, a poor ignorant child.

Translated by LADY MACFARREN.

Everything that they do themselves seems insignificant to them—and what others do appears immense. Megalomania lurks within them and they are consumed with envy. They all have one point at which they can touch greatness. They have dreams in which megalomania runs riot. They are able to fly, and they raise themselves proudly above the gazing crowd. Or they have done some great work, and the whole world is admiring them. There are not a few poets amongst these timid ones, who feel themselves so small and would like so much to be great. All the poet's Ego feelings seek an outlet and urgently demand release. He must therefore have an inward mental image of each of his visions. All dark demons of Hell and all good spirits of Heaven must wrestle in his breast. He must be able to hate violently and to love intensely; and it is always a portion of his own Ego which he loves—or which he hates.

The whole world is interpenetrated with our Ego-rays. We find a person unsympathetic if he brings before our eyes our own bad qualities in caricature. We hate any one when he personifies an unpleasant part of our soul.

This law not only holds good for the individual, but also for large communities, for whole nations. It is only by reason of this law that long æons of existence are rendered comprehensible to us. Why does the American hate the Negro? Just let us think out of what material the American population of to-day has been moulded. There were criminals, the flotsam and jetsam of life, ne'er-do-wells, aimless wanderers, psychopaths with strongly marked criminal instincts. These instincts were repressed, and a people developed with high morals and ethics, whose practical sense of acquisition is in glaring contrast with its mental ideals. What repression had to take place before this had been accomplished! The American has not freed himself from his evil instincts any more than we in the old world; on the contrary they rage more powerfully in his breast than he will confess to himself. It is the endeavour of all human beings to project unpleasant endopsychic observations outwardly. In short, that which we find unpleasant *in ourselves* we project on *to others*. The Negro stands as a representative of that which is evil in the American; in the Negro the American hates and despises himself. We could also find a similar foundation for Anti-semitism. We are all greedy for money, and eager for great wealth. We are idealists, in whom the business man has to yield unwillingly to the demands of ethics. We would like to rise above ourselves, and to climb to pure heights, but we can only do that when we separate that which is disagreeable in us and transfer it to another.

Without a scapegoat we cannot live; one needs magnanimity of soul to be one's own scapegoat. Thus we hate whole nations because they represent one of those components of our Ego which has been doomed to repression.

From this we can see the tremendous importance of vanity. There is no human being without vanity, and he who is least vain still prides himself on the fact that he is not vain. Who knows if the poet in the fairy tale did not pose as the man without vanity in order to represent himself as the only being of a different type to the ordinary mortal? That is the great secret of the ego-rays. Each person creates a world for himself, and is proud of it because it is his own world. In his innermost soul there reigns a self-conceit which will endure no comparisons. Who has not conceived the dream of being the only survivor of the downfall of the world? If only people would know that they are all "unique" and that a community of human beings can never produce a unity! If we look a little more closely we see nothing but ego-rays which are at war with each other—an eternal chaos out of which will eventually be born the eagerly desired world of altruism.

CHAPTER II

THE FIGHT OF THE SEXES

LOVE is the poetry of those who are not poets. That mood which we call " poetic " is very readily created whenever there is an undercurrent of erotic emotion. People in love are always " poetic "; they wander enchanted in the rosy twilight of a land of dreams, for all reality appears to them far away and impossible, because dream is for them reality.

The true poet can create these moods out of the smallest happenings of everyday life, without himself being in love. Everywhere he is able to see problems and conflicts where other mortals see only grey monotony; but Love sees no problems, and sustains itself by moods of unsatisfied longing.

Love stands at the beginning of a happy marriage. Happiness is to make outside interests one's own interests. Only lovers (not merely the "loving") can do this. The lover identifies himself with the object of his love, while the merely "loving" has still preserved a remnant of his Ego, and his own interests remain.

Every marriage is founded on some common interest, if it be only the erotic relationship, for this is certainly an interest in common—and not the least important.

Many observers have been struck by the fact that marriages of love are not the most happy ones, or only in the rarest cases. How does that come about? One might believe that instinct is the surest guide for love. Yes, and for *love* it is the best guide. But love and marriage are not the same thing. We must first explain the riddle of love. One need not smile. There are many more riddles in everyday life than we imagine. Already the theme of love's choice challenges the keen penetration of the psychologists, and even more so does the whole problem of love.

What a strange schematic conception of love have we hitherto had! There has always been something enigmatic and inexpressible about it. It strikes man like a flash of lightning; it makes him blind to the light of experience, and deaf to every voice of reason. For to love means to feel—and where feelings rule, the intellect become a hopeless slave.

Now we human beings are so formed that we will not admit to ourselves that we are driven to this or that action merely by an obscure and incomprehensible feeling. We always seek intellectual grounds, " rationalization," for our emotional life, and bring our thoughts to bear upon our feelings. So the lover discovers in his Beloved all possible and impossible good qualities, in order to excuse his love to himself. These good qualities, however, collapse like a house of cards, when the emotion of love disappears, and the eye then, made keen by hate, magnifies the faults that had hitherto been so easily and so willingly overlooked.

Now I speak of hate, who have just been speaking of love. Is there, then, a love that can also hate?

There is in human life no emotion which is not conjoined with, and kept in equilibrium by, an opposite emotion, nor impulse, by an opposite impulse. This phenomenon is best explained by an example from the organic world. Our health is assured by a system of glands, several of which play the rôle of antagonists. The one gland excretes a substance which would become poison if it were not made harmless by the excretions of another gland. If one of these glands is removed, illness invariably arises in consequence of the excessive excretion from the other gland; unless it be that a third gland comes to the help, and takes over the rôle of the antagonist. It is so with our impulses. Our various desires act upon one another like clockwork. Every desire is opposed by another desire, which holds it in check. It is an eternal ebb and flow, whereby sometimes the one, sometimes the other desire gets the upper hand. Everything in human life is "bi-polar." *

There is no love without hate; and there is no hate without love. The opposite of love is not hate, but indifference; the opposite of feeling can only be the absence of feeling. Disinclination, which is coloured by feeling, often only serves the purpose of concealing and protecting oneself against an inclination. Love and hate must go hand in hand; and the people we love most we hate also, because hate is grounded in the nature of love. "*Plus on aime une maîtresse, plus on est près de la haïr,*" says La Rochefocauld.

Of course we have to consider one thing, this hate will never show itself openly; its existence will work underground, accumulate, pour forth in dreams, until it openly breaks out at the first opportunity, immense and overpowering, and we face the phe-

* I have thoroughly explained this "Law of Bi-polarity" in my book *Die Sprache des Traumes* (Verlag J. F. Bergmann, Wiesbaden, 1911).

nomenon overwhelmed and helpless, owing to the elemental and irresistible power of the emotion.

After this explanation it will be more easily understood when I assert that between the sexes there exists a ceaseless conflict, which I call " the strife of love." The strongest tendency of man is, as Nietzsche so very aptly expressed it, his "will to power." Every human being wants to rule, every one wants to be king, at least in his youth, before relentless time has bowed his back and accustomed him to servitude. This mania in people for ruling is never shown more clearly than in a small circle. Just let us watch what a bitter and ridiculous fight takes place in small circles for the ruling power. He who cannot rule at home tries his luck outside in the world, and becomes the leader of a society; but eventually is himself deposed through the " will to power " of his friends.

I have seen family tragedies which have had their roots in this " will to power." And through what insignificant causes! I remember specially one case where a mother-in-law and her daughter-in-law hated to do the housekeeping together. A most bitter feud arose between the two women as to who should give the orders to the servant girl. (A very banal and common example; but it better illustrates my assertions than the noblest that I could find.) If the younger woman had arranged for the washing to be done on Tuesday, the elder one saw in that a decline of her rights of ascendency, and decided for Friday instead; when, on the other hand, the elder woman had arranged to have veal and potato soup for to-morrow's dinner, then the young one rebelled, and tried to get beef and spaghetti. Both orders rained down on the head of the servant, and the son (and husband) had to play the part of judge. One would be tempted to smile over these little comedies, if they did not so frequently change into tragedies. The young one died of these trivialities. She " bled inwardly," as she ceased to discuss it with her husband; for she did not want to vex him. Why do we always seek for great heroic motives for the tragedies in life? Often great motives lead to small deeds, and small affects have often caused the greatest events. To such struggles noble hearts sacrifice their best powers. But we need strife. Without struggle existence is impossible. When the opportunity for strife is lacking, then begins the fight against our own self. The " will to power " is generally wrecked on this hard-hearted Ego. Self-control is the most difficult thing for man to learn.

But let us return to our theme. The " will to

power" never leaves the individual. If he cannot use it in great circumstances in the outer world, he will employ it in a smaller way. Every one must have something to exercise mastership over, even though it be only a dog or an errand-boy. Alas, that children must so often be sacrificed to this inveterate desire for mastership, under the pretext of a good education! "Good education" is often enough only an excuse to show power.

But how far have I travelled from love? Nevertheless, I was on the right way. I only wanted to show how a person when he falls in love, so deeply in love that he grows blind to all the other's faults and magnifies the good qualities, then recognizes this other as his conqueror, as the unquestioned ruler over his feelings, and for love of him, or her, renounces the "will to power." The lover subjects himself to his beloved object. The "will to power," however, has not been broken, but only repressed. Hate, which follows this suppression of individuality, is thrust below the threshold of consciousness and kept far from the light of day. This subjection to the will of another carries in itself the germs of revolt. Hatred nourishes itself upon the little suggestions of faults observed in the other, and grows stronger and expands until it threatens to burst the locks of its prison. It seeks an outlet. It unites itself with the "will to power" and carries on a silent and therefore all the more bitter fight against love. This is the reason why this pathological condition of being in love has to come to an end. We are not able to roam always on the heights of ecstasy. We need the depths just as much as we require the heights. Disillusion must follow intoxication, and new intoxication must follow disillusion. An eternal see-saw is the game the soul and its powers play.

And so begins in love the silent fight of the sexes for mastership. There is no compromising. There is only an "either—or." Hammer or anvil is the great question of every marriage. In marriage, hatred finds new food, because the strongest inclination in the human being, his "will to power," is actually the will to independence. It is not without reason that people talk so much of freedom, and make such great sacrifices for it. Personal freedom is, and remains, our greatest ideal. It is merely the expression of an impulse which one might call the impulse for independence. Really every one is an anarchist in the depths of his nature; every being is to himself the "unique." And all the submission which civilization demands from us, the giving up of the personality and of independence, the fitting in with the community—all this is sacrifice. So also is marriage a sacrifice. We sacrifice our polygamous instincts for the glory and welfare of one being. We sacrifice willingly, at least we think so; but within man, where the bad instincts sleep (or shall we not rather call them the most ancient, perhaps even the truly primaeval instincts of man?) a secret something revolts against this sacrificing of the personality; it begins to make use of hatred, and forces its way through dark secret channels towards the surface.

Thus every marriage is a secret struggle between man and wife, a fight which is never fought out to the point where extremes meet. It is these victories in small affairs which stand as symbols for more important matters. A happy marriage is that where the fight is ended by the total submission of one party. Or the sphere of rule for each is fixed after many weary struggles between both parties, and thus a compromise is created, a kind of equation, against which dissatisfied opposing elements continually rebel. In no marriage is this struggle entirely at rest. The most peaceful of marriages are like the modern " World Peace "; it is an armed peace. This love struggle explains the enigma of many phenomena of life. We often meet wives of men of importance who never recognize the greatness of their husbands, and who are their most severe critics. We find men who never consider their wives beautiful, although they may be admired by the whole world, because they are their own. We see also that marriages are wrecked because people love each other too much, and yet neither wants to submit to the other.

This fight of the sexes extends into social life, and is to-day more violent than ever. How all the male world revolted when women claimed for themselves that holy symbol of manhood, trousers! What a bitter fight did the suffragettes put up in London for that scrap of power which suffrage gives to them! The fight of the sexes has assumed grotesque proportions since it has been carried over from the love region into the social region.

We do not know yet what the future will bring. Woman has been too long suppressed, and has been forced to obey, and in the course of thousands of years such hate has been stored up as must break forth with explosive force and destroy everything which bars its way. The power which now smashes a window pane, or pulls a policeman from his horse, is the strength accumulated from the inglorius past, from which only a fairy tale of an Amazon kingdom has been handed down to us. How grand must these women be in their love when they can hate thus! And how far are they from the knowledge which we have gained from our reflections!—"I hate you because I love you so, and I love you because I hate you so."

It is clear from the Law of Bi-polarity that this fight will never end, for in this struggle there can neither be victor nor vanquished. Every defeat is at the same time a victory, which garlands the defeated with red roses; and every victory is paid for with bitter tears. This is the ancient fairy tale of the fight between the Gods and the Giants. It is knowledge wrestling with the impulses. Unfortunately every one has his hour when he must experience his "twilight of the gods." Every love, however great, has an end. It is the sign of greatness in people when they acknowledge that, and let great feelings die in beauty. It would appear then to be a condition for happiness in marriage to approach it with a certain kind of resignation. Or should one prepare oneself more thoroughly for this conflict, and struggle in good time against one's own fighting Ego?—in order to reduce one's demands to an honourable peace, in which there is really neither victory nor defeat? So many incidents play an important part in this question, which for reasons easily to be understood I cannot explain. It is now almost a commonplace that the erotic union needs also an agreeing of the erotic tendencies, but this is still easily forgotten when marriage is in question. The more strongly the erotic power is in evidence, the stronger also is the part it plays in marriage, and the more easily it leads to that destructive fight which I have tried to describe. This secret fight of the sexes plays an especially great part in sexual relationship. I know many people who evade the fulfilment of their love because it would mean the entire submission and giving up of their individuality. Hebbel, most genial of poets, and unsurpassed psychologist, has expressed this most excellently in his drama *Judith*. Judith, who loved Holofernes as much as she hated him, says to Mirza ". . . That he hauled me off with him, forced me to his shameful bed, stifled my very soul—all that you suffered. And now, when I will have payment for the annihilation that I tasted in his arms—now, when I will revenge myself for that brutal blow at my individuality—now, when I will wash off in his heart's blood the defiling kisses that still scorch my lips . . . oh, do you not blush for shame to urge me hence?"* She must kill Holofernes in order to extinguish her shame. She feels her sexual surrender as a defeat of her personality; she thinks only about herself, and sees herself become "smaller and smaller till she disappears into nothing."

We shall be able to understand one of the diseases of our time. We shall understand that there are neurotics who shrink from every love as from one which might put them in bonds, because they are afraid of the domination of one outside themselves—the deepest cause of many hindrances in the capacity to love! . . .

To give oneself entirely to another means to give oneself up, to lose one's self. I know a highly refined intellectual woman who belongs to two men. One makes her feel all the joys and glories of sexuality. In his arms she "becomes nothing" and melts away. And she bathes herself in it, according to her own expression, as in a rejuvenating spring, making her feel well for weeks after. But she hates this man and flees his presence, because his every embrace is like a defeat for her. On the other hand, she loves an artist enthusiastically, but his embraces leave

*I am indebted to Mr. Bertram Lloyd for this passage from his forthcoming translation of Hebbel's *Judith*.

her entirely cold. In this example she, being the ruler, can feel only the ecstasies of ruling.

This fight between eroticism and sexuality, between the sexual craving and psychic penetration, is a disease of the time. Amiel Lucka talks in his fine spirited work of the "Three Grades of Eroticism"; of the first grade, purely sensual love, of the second as purely spiritual love, and of the third grade an intermixing of sensuality and spiritualized love. This third stage is the goal of all more highly differentiated civilized people. But how few are the chosen ones who reach this ideal! The cultured person would have to sustain his love through an endless series of disappointments for the fulfilment of this longing. It is but a very rare chance when marriage also means this fulfilment. Where it is so, the fight may cease and hatred retire for ever.

One can understand the love tragedies of those unhappy people who have found this ideal but cannot realize it. One can understand dying of love, when cruel life denies love its highest fulfilment.

Most people have to reduce their demands to moderation. They have to be satisfied either with the sexual fulfilment or with the intellectual bond. Sexuality or eroticism, that is the end of our wanderings in search of the third stage of love.

But how to fight the difficulties in such a case, how to steer round the dangerous cliffs, when the mind revolts against the body, and when the body refuses obedience to the mind? How is it possible to achieve in such compromised marriages a state of peace where the struggle of the sexes will be at least apparently appeased? In such a case only self-knowledge and the rich field of great mutual interests can help. We are choked by trifles as in a sea of sand. We all suffer through trivialities, and lose thereby the capacity to rejoice in big things and to grasp them in their full greatness.

The happiness of marriage rests on the capability of persistently overlooking trifling objects, and of focussing one's lust of fighting upon the world at large. Great aims produce great people. One must not demand everything from love, one must not over-estimate one's own love. Love cannot do everything, even though one may believe that it could remove mountains. Such a love is very rare. We are no longer capable of heroic feelings; the time of heroes is past. Small people have small feelings—but one can still be happy with small feelings if one contents oneself with them. Many marriage soups cannot get warm because one puts too big pots on a small fire.

But to those fortunate ones who have found their

bodily and mental complement life blossoms in its richest colours. They do not know the humiliation of submission, nor the triumphs of ruling. They have achieved the great miracle, to win and to be defeated, to obey and to command, and from two beings have become one dual being, which holds every possibility of the future.

CHAPTER III

AIMS IN LIFE

Who does not, in his innermost soul, envy the man who journeys with unfaltering steps towards a definite aim, whose strivings and endeavours represent a fight for an unchangeable goal, and who, after having attained his aim, enjoys, serene and satisfied, the fruits of his labour? All actions are co-ordinated into a complete unity by a well-controlled mind; every energy is centred upon one idea, and the whole aim is reflected in every little part, clearly and distinctly. Now let us look, on the other hand, at people who have no aim! How vacillating is their will, how powerless their actions! To-day they believe they have discovered their vocation, and to-morrow they are already tortured by doubt; that which they have accomplished seems valueless and not worth the trouble spent upon it, and the thing really worth striving for in the far distance. Their life is a continual wavering, a going backwards and forwards, and a yielding and a rushing on. The goal changes, disappears, reappears, sometimes gigantic and within reach, at others enveloped in far distant mist like a Fata Morgana, a will-o'-the-wisp which lures to death and destruction. . . .

We must occupy ourselves with the children if we want to make observations about the life aims of people. Children all dream of great aims. And all the different aims of different people disclose one endeavour—to uplift oneself above others, to enforce one's personality, and to rule. This strongest power in our soul, the "will to power," erects before our eyes such a powerful and sublime aim in life, so far over-towering the common world, and so uplifting that no reality can ever reach it.

The secret of the whole art of life is . . . to be able to renounce. Everybody has somewhat to reduce his childish aim, which allures him so immensely and entices him so far, to a measure which is attainable. He must diminish the distance, and shift the goal nearer the attainable, and sacrifice his childish dream bit by bit to a cruel reality. He must lose the belief in his "great historical mission." Every person counts himself as quite exceptional. Every one, in his innermost soul, strongly fights against being submerged in the great crowd and becoming one stone amongst many. Every one endeavours to rise up, to strive to the heights, to shine, gain fame, acquire wealth, kindle the envy of others, and feel himself as the moving power in the whirring machine of life. Education fosters this belief in a great mission. Parents who have realized that they themselves will never be able to attain their ideals, want to conquer death in their children and so gain immortality. Every mother has dreams that her child will attain to something "very exceptional." Early signs of talent, so frequently in children only a sign of uneven mental development, are pointed out as prophecies of future greatness to the whole family, to visitors, and, what is worse, to the child itself. Thus the secret false belief of the child is justified by actual facts, and the aim of life so immensely elevated that the attainable reality can never be accomplished. This psychic root is the cause among others of countless suicides among children. Every suicide of a young person is a failure of his "great historical mission," and at the same time a more or less justified protest against the overweening pride and incapacity of the educator who failed to instil attainable and reasonable aims of life in the young soul.

For a long time there has been no agreement as to

the nature of nervousness. Now we have already penetrated deeper into physic connexions with neurosis, and we have unravelled the secret interplay of the impulses. We know the hell of hate and envy which boils in the soul of one who is disappointed and deceived in his aim in life. "Neurosis is the dirge of a broken-down ambition, illuminated only by the pale moon of envy," as I defined neurosis in my book, *Die Träume der Dichter* (Verlag J. F. Bergmann, 1912). The dreams of poets were especially valuable to me, because they all manifested the wrestling ambition and the secret belief in a great aim of life. "All poets dream that they can fly, and that they can raise themselves high above common mortals. They converse in their dreams with gods, and they seem to be gifted with supernatural powers. God appears to them as to the elect. Sometimes He threatens in the shape of a cloud, or shines like a firebrand into the soul, at others His voice sounds in warning, urging and calling to great deeds." In their dreams the poets converse with kings and important personages. Napoleon rides through their dreams, Christ preaches to them, and miracles take place under their influence.

The poet has set up for himself a definite aim in

life. He is seeking fame, immortality. He wants to instruct people, to educate them, and to become an apostle of beauty. All his productions manifest this aim in life, to which but few attain though many strive. This enables us to get some understanding of the would-be poets. The aim in life is the same, but the powers give out. They believe in themselves, and no critic can persuade them that they do not belong to the elect. They suspect everywhere ill-favour, cliques, ill-luck; they strive for protection, they beg and humble themselves only in order to get nearer to their aims in life, and thus to triumph over their fellow beings. Those who act thus are mostly neurotic, soul sick, because they cannot keep in check the inward onward-urging power. Slaves to an impotent ambition.

We have arrived then at our theme, the life aim of the neurotic! All those people have no definite aim in life, and the dissatisfaction with their work is common knowledge. The lawyer envies the doctor, the doctor the lawyer, the business man the student, the professor the business man; each one declares that if he could live his life in the world again he would not choose his present work—rather would he break stones! That is the favourite phrase, which no one takes seriously. The beautiful old custom that the son should take over the vocation of the father, his business, his practice, is quite the exception to-day. The sons of business men become poets, the sons of painters become photographers, and the sons of poets become officers. That proves that they are all disappointed, and that their vocation and their aim in life do not agree. We find at the present time more people who change their vocation than ever before. Young people who study first the law and then medicine, to end finally in journalism; doctors who become musicians, poets who become manufacturers, and manufacturers who go on the stage. Some change so often that finally they are without any work at all. It seems as if a secret power would urge them to excel and to lift themselves above the mediocrity of everyday life. Let us not forget those unhappy ones who devote themselves to art. Anæmic girls go trembling on the stage and sing songs with a shaky voice to attain notoriety; legions of touring pianists, violinists, reciters, painters and so on. I do not speak of the really exceptional ones, of whom there are so few. But to-day an endless proletariate of art throws itself on the stage, with an army of kind acquaintances willing to applaud each favourite. The critics are dragged by hook or by crook to the concert-hall for the sake of a dream of fame, which usually ends up with the honourable career of a teacher . . . with a few withered laurel leaves, and generally a most splendidly bound book which contains the collected criticisms of the Press, amongst which the flattering critic of one obscure provincial paper confirms the pride of the family.

All those who watch with seeing eyes this bitter struggle for the smallest step, the smallest rising step, will mark the power of human ambition. The driving force in all these people is the secret belief in their Ego, the belief that they are of the elect. All art proletariates are neurotics, but a healthy, sane man can never so entirely lose his power of self-criticism.

Neurosis exhibits besides these openly apparent forces some secret tendencies which are veiled to consciousness. It shows a very subtle construction; it shows a bewildering interplay of the impulses for the sake of a secret aim in life. Only through knowledge of this aim do we get the key to the neurosis, and the tangle of psychic powers is unravelled. Perhaps I had better give again an example to make myself understood. A lady suffered for thirty years from the well-known phenomenon which we call "agoraphobia." It is impossible for her to go out alone, and on her bad days she cannot even go accompanied by several people. Neither can she go in any underground place. When she wants to go to a theatre, the steps must lead upwards: she stood in Vienna in front of the Coliseum for half an hour, and could not go in because the steps led downwards. She liked the Burg Theatre because she could mount up to it. On investigation of the cause of the phobia one discovered a wish to protect herself from the dangers of the bad world. This lady felt herself safest at home. But this does not explain the strange phenomenon of fear of the deeper lying localities; for she could not go into any cellar, and no amount of money would ever have induced her to visit a mine. Her neurosis showed a distinct ascetic tendency. She had been for many years a vegetarian, was abstinent, and had also given up the smoking of cigarettes. Previously, she had liked to read books, but she also had to renounce this pleasure. A hysterical disturbance of sight hindered her from reading.

Psycho-analysis gave the explanation of these strange phenomena. She held the secret belief that she would gain a good place in heaven by all this renunciation. Of what value to her were all the successes and joys of this world when she could hear in her dreams the hosannas of the angels, when she could converse with the saints, and was surrounded by the splendour of heaven? The fear of cellars resolved itself into fear of hell, which is placed below in people's imagination. In spite of the fact that she read Nietzsche daily, and worshipped Haeckel, one can hardly believe that this patient was unaware of her secret piety. Innumerable are those pious people who believe in their hearts, and are outwardly freethinkers.

This patient had also found a secret aim in life. She was first driven by a burning ambition to become something very remarkable. Her belief in her "mission" in this world seemed unshakable. Then the proud hopes fell to the ground with crippled wings, one after the other; the rich marriage, the prince who was to fetch her in his golden carriage, her great talents, which failed of fruition in her life, the child who was to be a wonder. . . . There remained only hope in the other world, which she called the "eternal" one. She built castles in the air where her dreams should find fulfilment. Her longing for the bliss of heaven corresponded to her fear of the horrors of hell.

We know to-day that we cannot heal a neurotic until we have discovered his hidden aim in life. Certain definite ways lead to this aim, which Alfred

Adler has called very aptly " guiding lines." These guiding lines lead, according to this author, to " godlikeness "—as I would call it, to heaven. And the artful construction which the neurotics have built themselves in order to gain their great aim, one might call with Adler the " neurotic fiction." As a protection against the crushing feeling of inferiority they build themselves edifices of neurosis. It is for this reason that the neurotics are so unwilling to give up their disease. They feel they are safe in it, as is a snail in its house. To retire into oneself, to live only for oneself, to give a wide berth to the defeats of the outside world, that is the endeavour of all patients. Most neurotics belong to this type; they all had a time when they strove for the highest aims, and dreamt of getting on well in the world. They wanted to uplift themselves high above the average mortal, and their flight went to the highest stars. Then came the great bankruptcy, and their great fantasies, all the beautiful plans of a great future, dissolved. There remained finally only one hope, life after death. There were still all the possibilities open to them if the remaining part of life was well used. . . .

In addition, there is a second very strange phenomenon. All neurotics suffer from an agonizing feeling of guilt. Being pious inwardly, they are afraid of punishment from heaven. I have explained elsewhere that every fear is fear of the punishment of God.

It is the final great examination, the Last Judgment, of which the neurotics are afraid. They continually dream of examinations for which they are not properly prepared. These exams are exams before God, and Matriculation is a symbol for the passing of the Judgement Day Examination. Some dream that they have to pass an exam in religion; the examiner is a kind, or a severe, old gentleman, a professor, or one of the other figures of youthful fear behind which is hidden, God. The whole neurosis is thus a preparation for the great examination. All ascetic strivings, all tortures, all sufferings of nervous people, have only this one meaning: to punish themselves in this earthly life. Harmless misdeeds in youth, the well-known childish errings, are dragged to light by the searching anxiety of conscience, the only result of which is to make the fear of joy in life the most important life principle. Every pleasure is counted as a sin and every affliction as a just punishment. Of course the neurotic remains unconscious to all these psychic impressions. He has pushed his aim in life far out into another world, and is striving towards this aim in life as if he were dominated by a fixed idea.

Here a wide field is opened for educational application. Away with all exaggerated demands upon our children, which are only the expression of our own presumption! Let us educate them to be modest and satisfied! Let us show them aims which their ambition can reach, and let us fill their souls with conceptions which can be fulfilled. Let us teach them the most difficult and most important thing: renunciation.

Then the wondrous flower of Joy-in-Life will blossom for them. They will not be devoured by futile envy, by bitter impotence, and the crushing feeling of their own inferiority.

I would like to conclude these deductions with a few splendid sentences by Otto Ludwig, which I have taken from the book called *Gedanken*, published after his death. May every one who despairs of attaining his aim in life read them very carefully, and take them to heart!

" The idealism of young people is vanity. With a certain arbitrariness, youth can become enthusiastic about everything, if he only brings it in relation to his vanity. And what is more gratifying to his vanity than the sublime scorn with which he is looking down on actualities and human affairs from the height of a flattering self-deception, as being something vulgar? He demands great deeds from others, not because he himself is doing them—no—but because he thinks himself capable of doing them." "Scepticism, if it comes after enthusiasm, and is born out of it as an opposite, is the growing pains of our inner being, and the condition necessary for development. We must despair of our imagined value in order to become conscious of our real one. What a person previously demanded from others without knowing if he himself could do it, that he himself will now do without demanding it from others."

"*The highest aim to which he could reach was to die for something gloriously; now he has raised himself to a greater height—to live for something without fame.*"

CHAPTER IV

MALI-MALI

THERE is found in the Philippine Islands a peculiar illness which is called by the natives "Mali-Mali." Whilst the rich in our country often suffer from a form of nervous irritability which we call "tic," "Mali-Mali" is the illness of poor people. There is nothing strange in that. We recognize nowadays the significance of the social influence of the surroundings in the origin of disease. We know that every country has its own illnesses, that every vocation produces some typical diseases (occupation disorders). A new branch of medicine, so-called social medicine, is occupied with the investigation of these conditions.

So "Mali-Mali," an illness of the poor, is a special form of those disturbances which we have hitherto *called wrongly*—"nervous" disturbances. It is a disturbance of the psychic life, to express ourselves in a more modern and precise way: the French have called it very suitably "psychasthenia"—"soul weakness." Such poor men or women as suffer from "Mali-Mali" show the following most peculiar symptoms. They have to imitate everything that is done by the person (there may be several in one day), under whose influence they happen to be at a given moment. If their "pattern" looks up at the sky, the "mimics" will also look up at the sky. If he bends down to pick up something from the ground, the mimic will do the same. If he then says indignantly "Thou art a fool," then the mimic repeats "Thou art a fool!" These people will go on doing this until the model they have chosen relieves them from the spell, and forbids them to copy everything. If the "Ideal" will have a joke with the poor sufferer, they will jump to it unhesitatingly. They will follow him like a shadow, and will imitate slavishly what he performs. If they should lose their model, they will quickly choose another one; for the "Mali-Mali" sufferer cannot exist without an ideal and model.

One can easily imagine what a pitiful existence these people lead, deprived of all self-determination. They are incapable of any kind of work, except with an example to copy from. They can only eat when their Ideal does, and even involuntary functions are fulfilled, not according to their own need, but according to the example of their Ideal. We are astonished at this peculiar type of psychic disturbance, which is unknown in this unmitigated degree in any other part of the world. We do know of some similar phenomena, such as echolaly of the insane and of the hysterical. Echolalysts repeat every word one tells them. We also remember that children sometimes show the symptoms of echolaly, and that a tendency to "Mali-Mali" is not rare in children's games. We might even prove that "Mali-Mali" exists in a very marked form in Europe, and that we could with good cause occupy ourselves a little more thoroughly with this mental epidemic.

Let us consider first how such a strange illness can arise. What is the power which can deprive the psychic machinery of all impulse of its own? We get an important indication from the fact that the illness is confined to poor people, and that it is the rich people whom they select for their adulation. This fact itself gives us some insight into the meaning of this form of Mali-Mali, already familiar to us in our own country. Poor people with us also ape the rich, and adopt their customs, manners and dresses. One might even remark that all our servants suffer from Mali-Mali. They use their small wages to adorn themselves for their few hours of leisure in order to look like their mistress. They wear large, ridiculous hats, exactly similar to those of their mistress; and, if possible, fashionable coats, gloves, and patent leather shoes in imitation of her, in accordance with Mali-Mali's demands.

Why do I speak only of servants, and do not mention that our bourgeois classes also irrevocably suffer from Mali-Mali? Let us be under no illusion: the difference between rich people and the middle class is to-day entirely wiped out. The wife of the small official must have her silk petticoat to rustle through the streets. The cheap hat is a fable from times long gone by, and the absurd monster which wobbles on the head, fixed by means of countless hat-pins and ribbons, devours the fourth part of a month's salary (unless Mali-Mali has had the effect of the mad luxury being paid for by a "third party" at a sacrifice of all good principles).

The primitive people of the Philippines exhibit a common human phenomenon in a specially deceptive and naïve form. We cultured people can hide our weaknesses so much more cleverly, and attribute to free will much which is in reality only the effect of Mali-Mali. A poor Malay in this condition grows up with the tremendous respect which the poor have for the rich. The wish in him to become a rich person and to bear himself in a distinguished manner at length grows so strong that it destroys such little individuality as he possesses, and compels him to seek an ideal for himself. Are we any better or more reasonable than he is? This illness betrays the lack of self-reliance of so many people. We believe we choose freely and decide according to our own judgement. But when we look into it a little more closely we find that we are actuated by Mali-Mali. Nothing is more difficult than to go one's own way and to be an independent personality. We are under the compulsion of fashion, which is only Mali-Mali in another form. Woe to the person who tries to oppose this tyrant! Aesthetic sense and comfort are subordinated to the dictum, "One wears now only this or that." How few women have the courage to defy the Mali-Mali fashion? And how few lords of creation? Yes, let us admit openly; we men are just as much subject to Mali-Mali as are women. What ridiculous leaps Art performed when first seeking emancipation! What shall we say of those incredible insanities of the cubists and futurists, who have also produced their ape-like imitators! And were there not thousands and thousands who lost their own reason and their own taste, and went into raptures when they saw grass-green, grey-violet daubs, and spoke ecstatically of a new era in Art? Grinning gargoyles, which were intended to enhance the picturesqueness of our town, threatened us from the façades of our houses! Mali-Mali was diligently at work, and the few sensible people were shouted down.

We get a most striking example of the great power of Mali-Mali in the development of cycling. There was a time when cycling was exclusive to the upper classes. Aristocrats and heads of affairs accustomed every fine morning to their ride in the open. How healthy that was for all the different people in offices! They got up early and went to bed early. They spent two hours in the clean air, had some exercise, and went with renewed vigour to their sedentary work.

Suddenly, cycling went out of fashion. Mali-Mali had spoken the decisive word, even in that. We do not cycle any more, because it is no longer considered fashionable. The motor-car has killed the bicycle. Cycling is no longer considered the vogue of the upper classes. It is, so to say, a sign of poverty, and means in the eyes of some people, "I am too poor to buy myself a car." It is an occupation which necessitates a good deal of exertion. It has always been a privilege of the rich to let other people work for them. " Poverty is no crime," says an old proverb. But proverbs sometimes need revision. They are continually repeated, but no one acts in accordance with them. We generally act as if poverty were a disgrace. Not only poverty, but also to be deprived of means and to have a small income seems to be a shameful thing; otherwise people would not try to create the appearance of being rich, and act as if they had wealth at their disposal. I have often noticed on trams that poor workmen and simple women give the largest tips. They only do it in order that the conductor may not think that they are unable to spare a few coppers. And are not those few coppers very often a great sacrifice for them?

It is as if everybody had only *one* anxiety and *one* care: that no one should know their poverty. Man is judged in our day, more than ever, by his exterior and by his behaviour. If people go to pleasure resorts, or on a holiday, their first question is, "Is the place frequented by high-class people?" Each tries to hob-nob with the better class in order to give the impression that he is also one of them. And these are supposed to be democratic times!

These Mali-Mali outgrowths reveal to us the whole misery of our psychic constitution! We have nothing in us which is really our own. We get our views from books and newspapers, our tastes prescribed for us by foreign people, and our hobbies are dictated by the fashion of the times. What remains then of our free will?

In short, Mali-Mali of the Malays shows us a common human phenomenon under the caricature of neurosis. Is neurosis anything other than a caricature of our weaknesses? We can demonstrate this in all the symptoms of a condition which we call neurotic. Nervousness is an over-emphasis of a human insufficiency.

There is a symptom which we call "weakness of will" (aboulia). The patient is incapable of making any decision. In extreme degrees the patient, for example, cannot get up in the morning because he cannot make the decision to leave his bed. Then he has to eat. What a hard, troublesome task! The nurse has to tell him to do it, and almost put the food in his mouth. And then dressing, going out, going to bed again and so on . . . ! All tremendously difficult tasks, which the patient despairs of being able to carry through. This illness, with which all civilization is permeated, is a caricature of weakness of will. All our education tends to suppress free will and to give us commands. People never learn to obey the commands of their own soul and of duty. They are always taught to copy the example of others. They are trained in childhood to imitate everything that is done before them. Our life is arranged according to samples. Unfortunately they are often samples without value!

I have often emphasized the fact, and I cannot repeat it too frequently, that education in independence is the most valuable gift with which to endow our children. All material possessions are transitory. Even our culture is valueless if we cannot make a proper use of it. Independence alone can help us over the difficulties of life.

We endeavour, by very carefully thought out educational principles, to educate our children up to Mali-Mali. Is it to be wondered at if they, when grown up, cannot renounce this weak habit of imitating? It is much easier, and much more convenient, to copy an example than to create. Behind Mali-Mali hides our greatest original sin—laziness. It is a particular form of laziness: laziness of will and of thought. Undoubtedly it is just as dangerous a form of laziness as any other.

What disaster this laziness of will and thought produces in political circles! The noblest spirits of the nation retire from the political battlefield. They frequently leave those places which should really belong to them to adventurous and professional makers of strife. And would those strifemongers have such an easy game if Mali-Mali did not bring them followers by the thousand? We talk in such cases of the power of suggestion. Suggestion is nothing else but a form of Mali-Mali. Somebody gives us an order, an opinion, a conviction, an affect, and we follow it blindly. We are quite incapable of coming to an independent apprehension of life and all its events, because we are brought to a stand-still by any extraneous opinion, and collapse before every exhibition of authority. All that is caused by Mali-Mali. Whoever wants to be free must first, by way of a "psychic anarchy," learn to rid himself of the despotism of the soul. In order to serve the God in our own soul, we must first destroy the idols of the false gods. But now we are confronted with the vexed question: What is real and what is false? What is the true God, and what are idols? The deplorable fact in the phenomenon of Mali-Mali consists in its being a necessary product of the conditions of our time. We need a great deal of authority in order to hold the animal in man in check. "I should like to know," says Lichtenberg, "what London would look like if one could, for ten minutes, do away with the Ten Commandments!"

We need the Commandments urgently—because unfortunately psychic anarchy is the beginning of social anarchy. Every period produces its institutions and its disorders. These disorders are the negative of the advantages. Obedience and fulfilment of duty are the highest virtues of the citizen. What virtue is there which does not have a limit, after which it becomes a vice? It seems to be the case that in human nature good cannot exist without its opposite. I have called this phenomenon, which can be traced through the whole psychic life, the "Law of Bi-polarity." Bi-polarity is also a phenomenon of Mali-Mali. The Beautiful and Good are thus spread abroad much more rapidly than by the more round-about way of conviction. So Mali-Mali also proves to be a power which must produce good. Think of the big deeds of charity, of all the rich gifts, of all the collections for a common cause, of all the noble endeavours of a really great personality, which are imitated by the great masses. And how often people come to love good and beautiful things for their own merit? First they are only apes, then pupils, and at last they become masters.

So we will not laugh any more about the Yellow Malays on the Philippine Islands when they run after people greater than themselves and imitate all their movements. Who knows if in the end they may not become really great themselves? And who knows that the woman suffering from Mali-Mali may not bear a child who, powerful, sublime, distinguished and brave, may become great, because his mother admired a great man? We, who have insight, should learn to be modest and to ask ourselves when we defend our ideas and our convictions: "Are they our possessions, or is it only Mali-Mali?" And I am afraid that only too often we have to think of the poor Malay, and to discover the secret model whom we have copied in our convictions. There is really no such thing as originality. All life is Mali-Mali. The secret lies in discovering a form which deviates to some little extent from the pattern. Everything new is but a variation of the old. There is also an anti-Mali-Mali, which is only a camouflaged form of Mali-Mali. There are people whose independence and originality consists in always doing the opposite; people who copy their ideal by an inversion into the opposite. From this kind of Mali-Mali let us guard ourselves most carefully! It gives us a delusive sense of independence and a dazzling appearance of originality.

Fashion is really an eternal vacillation between Mali and anti-Mali. In this vacillation between the opposites lies perhaps the secret of all progress. Fashion tries to hinder the change for a time. Vain endeavour! The stream rushes on, and we are carried away by it; we are driven while we think we are driving; we become changed, and we imagine that we produce change. Mali-Mali is eternal, and mocks all efforts at dethronement. The boundaries between Mine and Thine merge into each other, and there remains a fermenting, propelling, expanding, leavening mass, out of which the Powers of the Future are forming themselves.

CHAPTER V

HALF-MEN

THERE is at the present time a great longing for "Whole-Men." Any individual who proves himself to be such, may be sure of the appreciation of his contemporaries. Just remember the joy with which Nansen, Blériot and Amundsen were received! The whole world applauded them, an every one was in agreement in acclaiming them "Whole-Men." Their deeds were to all of us as the fulfilment of one of our own secret longings. We stood amazed and admiring before the phenomena of a gigantic will, steering without wavering towards its goal.

The prevailing disease of our time should be called, not neurasthenia, psychasthenia, hysteria or sensitiveness—but weakness of will. Every nervous disease can, of course, be traced back to the same psychic principle—the name does not matter much, it is but sound and smoke. But one is tempted to judge the problem of the diseases of our time in relationship to the will power, and to measure the weakness of the will power of the individual by the standards of his period. Some one might here remark that the present period has produced great men of strong will power. But extremes do not prove anything. It is the average which counts. That the longing to do a great deed may, in individual cases, result in a great deed being done, merely proves the exception and confirms the rule. Any one who knows our period must agree with me: "Whole-Men" are the exception—and "Half-Men" are unfortunately to be found in any number. "Half-Men" abound everywhere. Each tries many different occupations, and succeeds in none of them. One is half-artist—half-business-man; a second is half-official, half-explorer; a third is half-socialist, half-liberal, a fourth half-pious—half-atheist; a fifth half-Don-Juan, and half-philistine. And if only there were none *less* than "Half-Men!" There are countless characters divided into "thirds," "quarters," and even "tenths"; they split themselves up in different endeavours, and bring nothing to completion. Broadly speaking, the whole evil of our time may be described by the term "Half-Men."

We owe to Wernicke, the German Psychiatrist, the first communications about the dissociation of personality. Such persons create a different impression on different occasions. Like Proteus, they may appear in different forms, and express different views; and yet, in spite of contradictions, be perfectly sincere. It is always a partial Ego, a part only of the Ego, which expresses itself at one period, and naturally it has to express itself differently each time.

I will show in the following practical examples from life how these "Half-Men" behave themselves in contrast with "Whole-Men." A man in the prime of life, well-to-do, in a good position, with a good income, makes the acquaintance of a girl who fulfils all his expectations. Up to now he had resisted all temptations, and although he had met many beautiful women, none had become dangerous for him. He is now at the critical age, at the beginning of the forties, and he feels that he must come to a decision if he does not want "to miss the connexion," as the very apt saying goes. But his passion for the girl is continually held in check by his doubt. He questions himself over and over again: "Do I love her?" Doubt is already permeating this question. A lover need not put this question to himself; he knows and he feels that he loves. Our doubter tortures himself with these questions. When he is convinced that he does not love her, and decides to break with the girl, he becomes restless, and will soon reach a condition of utmost despair. But what if he really loves her and should lose her for ever? No, he cannot break with her, he will go and ask her to marry him. As soon as he arrives at her house, he discovers that her feet are too large. He ponders continually about the large unwomanly feet (they may not be large in reality, but he has arbitrarily chosen to see them thus), and tells the girl that he could never love her; she does not comply with his ideal of womanhood. On driving home, he is consumed by remorse. How could he have been so brutal? He immediately writes an urgent letter telling her not to take his words seriously, that he was beside himself, had spoken nonsense, and would like to talk with her again, etc., etc. Thus it can go on for a long while, and he cannot come to a decision.

Just recall the classical example: Grillparzer and Katharina Fröhlich! This is the way of "Half-Men!" Now how does the "Whole-Man" behave? He also has his scruples and doubts. But he can overcome them and arrive at a decision. We can only understand our "doubter" when we bear in mind that he is only a "Half-Man." One half urges him towards the woman, the other half is afraid of binding himself, and will hear nothing of marriage or bonds. Such people with dissociations of their psyche, are spoken of as weak characters, and as being unreliable. Their weakness of will is taken by the world as weakness of character. Therefore, many nervous people are taken for weak characters. Nothing is more ridiculous than the continual talk of weak and strong characters. Many a one who is taken for a weak character because he changes his views is really very strong, because he has the courage to see his error, to learn from it, and to take up a fresh point of view, in spite of knowing that he will be condemned for this very change. Another keeps to his point of view from cowardice, and from a kind of childish obstinacy, and figures as a strong character. It needs courage and an adequate training to listen to the urging of one's will. The words of the world-wise Rabelais: " Do what thou will'st," are only for those who know what they want. The sufferer from weak will does not know what he wants. This weakness of will can attain an extreme degree in neurotics. Let us again illustrate it by an example: A lady is lying lazily in bed and bemoaning her want of energy. She cannot get up. Getting up seems to her an insurmountably gigantic task. Then she must wash herself and comb her hair; all tremendous tasks. She has to be forced to do all these things. She needs an immense amount of time to get ready. At last, with much grumbling and groaning, she is able to finish. But with every new call upon her energy she has to face a new problem. She should go out, and cannot make up her mind to do so. Or she has to go to a theatre! The effort of will required to do this seems to her an extremely great and imposing thing. What if she is faced by something really great? Perhaps to find a new house or to change servants! Other people have to do that for her; she cannot summon such an act of will-power. We cannot arrive at the psychological significance of this condition of extreme weakness of will till we find, on investigating the origin of the illness, a suppressed wish, which troubled her at one time very much. (Of course, this is valid in this case, but not in all cases of "Aboulia.") Unfortunately she was unhappy in her marriage, and would have liked to leave her husband and to return to her parents. She knew that this would grieve her old mother, who was ill, and who was specially proud of the choice of this son-in-law. She could find no way out of this dilemma. She could not summon the strength of mind to take such an important step, fraught with so much excitement. That awful question, "What will people say to it?" prevented her from taking the step. She forced down her will, and consequently she lost her will-power. As she could not accomplish this *one step*, which would have given her freedom and happiness, so all other actions became valueless to her. What did she care about getting up and lying down, about theatres and a country house, compared with the one great question, the only question of her life? Her soul was obsessed by one idea only, and this idea was: "I cannot do it!" And everything she did and left undone reflected this terrible sentence, which contained all her tragedy, and wrecked all her life's happiness: "I cannot do it!" She was only a "Half-Person." One half was free and independent, and laughed at the world and its philistine views; the other half clung to the moral prejudices which she had received in her parental home. The second half became the stronger and suppressed the first, while the first took revenge and made her will powerless for all time.

The problem of the will is the central problem of life. Our patient lacked a central, overpowering will in the decisive question of her life. She lacked "the courage towards one's self." I wrote once in my booklet, *Ursachen der Nervösität* (Paul Knepler, Wien), "To own up to one's self is the beginning and end of a cure." And the well-known German psychologist, Marcinowski, had the splendid idea of calling his great work: "*Der Mut zu sich selbst*" (*Des Seelenleben der Nervösen und seine Heilung. Berlin: Verlag Otto Salle*, 1912).

He contends that weakness of will is a "loosening of the unity of the central Ego," and holds that: "it need not surprise us that our being is extremely complicated, and shows a tendency to split up into parts. We carry in us the life of our forefathers, or, more correctly speaking, themselves, as a heritage. In the end we are nothing other than the direct continuation of their life, and therefore we have within us not only those traditional "two souls," but fundamentally many souls. Happy he, whose separate souls, if we may so call them, urge chiefly in one direction. He will be able to remain healthy with a smaller expenditure of power."

Marcinowski gives a very apt comparison: "The power which we must presume to exist makes the organism appear to be a quite definite constitution. The more strongly this ruling power manifests itself, the more firmly and completely will the personality act when it enters the field of action. Its constitution is somewhat despotic, and its owner is likely to bring all conflicts of life to a dicision by a *coup d'état.*

The nervous person, on the other hand, resembles rather a state with a parliamentary constitution; with its struggles between different egoisms, individualities and party groups, with its elements of opposition and obstruction, with its strong and weak governments, its compromises and intrigues. This simile might be elaborated still further. That is how a nervous person appears, with his tendency towards a multiplicity of dissociations, with his internal tattered condition, and his external lack of a complete personality. Madness, so far as it is of a purely functional nature, would then be revolution and anarchy; the dissociation is then complete, and the State falls to pieces."

We therefore see that the "Half-Man" is in a condition similar to some states. He has to endeavour under all circumstances to reach a settlement by agreement if he wishes to live in peace. Only if he actually arrives at this settlement will he be equal to the demands of this life. In disharmony with himself, he has no energy available for the conflict of life. The "Half-Man" must therefore strive to become a "Whole-Man." But how? That is a difficult question to answer. The great secret of happiness and success is to find the middle path amongst all the contradictory influences of ethics, religion, duty and the ego impulses, without losing oneself and without transgressing the boundaries of the eternal laws. Marcinowski says: "It is the intention, not the deed, which shows the value in our actions. Therefore strive for the innermost, and the outward will come of itself. Strive earnestly that your thinking may agree with that Will, which nature reveals as the Will to Live, then your actions will be undistorted, and fully in agreement with each other." If I understand my colleague correctly, he would tell us: Courage towards oneself means the courage to know oneself, and knowing, to renounce many things. What would become of humanity if courage towards oneself should mean the courage to indulge all one's impulses? No! Courage towards oneself demands knowledge, and renunciation with open eyes. On the other hand, it does not demand renunciations performed out of cowardly considerations. We should be absolutely indifferent to what people say. We ought to stand high enough to be our own judges. The neurotic, too, stands in that position, but his severity is relentless. The criminal judges himself with too much leniency. The right way lies between the two. These problems are really for the educationists. It is a matter for those to whom young lives are entrusted, to form them into "whole" personalities. But it seems to me sometimes that the art of education is still in its infancy. First we must come to know the real man, so that we may be able to educate the Noble-Man, the man of the future. We are building on unsound foundations. Our education is a strange mixture of truthfulness and lies, courage and fear, morality and independence. The child hears: "Thou shalt not lie!" and the next moment Mother sends a message by the maid to the unwelcome visitor to say that she is not at home. Or the child is told not to be frightened, and to be courageous; but is warned repeatedly to beware of catching cold, to mind the trams, and motors, etc. Let us return to our examples. There we have the man who loves, and does not love, the girl, and who cannot come to a decision. We hear, however, that the girl possesses every virtue, but is poor. And our suitor is an idealist who pretends to despise money. Inwardly he is a great miser who wants to accumulate huge sums. He lies to himself and seeks other pretexts for his avarice. He has learnt this over-estimation of money in his parental home. He revolted against such a banal perception of life, but he could never overcome it. He had made up his mind only to marry a poor girl, but he always found faults with just those poor girls who came under his consideration. He was simply a " Half-Man." He should have been brought up in his youth to despise earthly riches. He should have learned that happiness is quite independent of the treasures we accumulate. And the woman who suffers from weak will has been brought up in an atmosphere where the opinion of the world was everything. She ought to have learnt that we should only listen to the voice of our heart, that we should do what seems good to ourselves, and then we should not mind anybody. She would then have become a "Whole-Personality." She would have found the courage to make her beloved parents understand that she could not live with her husband. She would have caused them less grief than by the severe illness which darkened the declining days of the careworn old people. And if the hesitating bridegroom had owned up to his lust for money instead of choosing the poor girl at all, he would not have been an ideal personality, but he would at least have been mentally sound. Or if the woman had formed a new marriage with the man she loved, although a child might have had to swing backwards and forwards between two marriages, she would have acted heartlessly towards the child, but the child would have had a healthy mother, and perhaps have been much happier. At anyrate, the two would have shown the "courage to oneself." They would have shown themselves as "Whole-Persons." But the possibilities are not exhausted. The woman's lot would have been better had she had full recognition of her own condition. Knowledge is never harmful. We must give our thoughts full freedom for development, they will then function as they ought. Marcinowski reminds us of a splendid sentence of Else Varnhagen: "Only complete freedom is really binding!"

Let us keep this before our eyes. Freedom of thought and courage towards oneself shall teach us to do good, not from fear of punishment, either earthly or heavenly, but from love of the good, from one's own free choice—without being forced or commanded. The "Whole Man" is only afraid of the judge in his own soul, and bows only before the commanded. The "Whole-Man" is only afraid of the future. Such books as the before-mentioned *Courage to Oneself* are produced to reconcile us with life, and to give us belief in this future. For one might despair at the unnecessary anguish and backwardness of humanity which still defends itself against enemies instead of seeking friends, which still divides instead of uniting, which still dreams of battles and streams of blood, instead of fêtes of joy and fraternization. One is almost ashamed of the word human being! It is a consolation to remember then that most human beings are only "one-third" —at the best "Half-Men." And who could expect a "*Whole*" civilization from "*Half*" Men?

CHAPTER VI

DOUBT

THE general character of the neurotic is dominated by two psychic phenomena; anxiety and doubt. While the former dwells in the foreground of consciousness, and occupies the most important position in every event, the latter, on the contrary, withdraws into the innermost recesses of the soul, and is so deeply hidden that its possessor is scarcely conscious of it. The number of doubters is infinite, but the number of those who recognize their doubt, and, more important still, admit the fact, is very small. Ibsen draws a distinction between healthy and morbid doubt, and says that he who doubts his own doubt is a morbid doubter. Hereby he draws a dividing line in the psychology of doubt which is not in accord with the facts. The doubter doubts everything, therefore he must also doubt his own doubt.

We see a similar phenomenon in the case of

anxiety. People suffering from any form of anxiety, for example, agoraphobia, eventually reach a state in which they suffer keenly from anxiety of anxiety; they fear they may be attacked by anxiety at critical moments. The layman can scarcely credit the diversity of these states of anxiety; and one cannot make an exact analysis of a neurotic without touching upon some of them. Anxiety appears in many different forms and masks—now it is anxiety about one's own health, now anxiety about the health of those dear to one; again it is anxiety about the uncertainty of the future, and, in serious cases, it amounts to "Pantaphobia," that is, anxiety about all and everything.

A thorough investigation always shows us that every anxiety turns out to be fear of oneself, and is always exhibited by those people who are afraid of themselves and of the evil impulses in their own breasts. I stated once: "Every neurotic is a criminal lacking the courage to commit crime." He is really afraid of his own suppressed criminal nature, and fears lest he might come in conflict with the law. He compensates his evil instincts by a hyper-moral character. He safeguards himself against his own criminal impulses. For instance, he dare not go in the street, and by this ensures his own safety; for then he cannot do anything wrong, and cannot come into conflict with the law. For example, a homosexual person, who does not know that he is homosexual, suffers from agoraphobia and cannot leave his house. Anxiety serves as a guard for his own virtue. He is the prisoner of his own Ego.

A similar phenomenon is doubt, which always goes hand in hand with fear. The fundamental root of doubt is doubt of oneself. *A person who believes in himself will never be a victim to doubt.* This does not prevent there being doubters who appear to be very self-conscious, and *seem* to be very satisfied with themselves and their good qualities. They only seem to be so. They sometimes play a part before themselves and before others. They act self-consciousness, and superiority, but deep in their souls a secret voice tells them: " You lie! You are acting a farce! Do you believe in all you profess? You are doubting!"

Is there then anything in which the doubter could believe? It is very striking that one cannot find a genuine believer who is a doubter at the same time. One of the causes of doubt is the struggle between the intellect and the emotions, between understanding and feeling. To the true believer, feeling and understanding have become identical; and the one thing which keeps him strong and helps him over all obstacles in life is what he calls his belief—belief in every form, it may be religion, science, politics or love. All strong belief disinfects the soul, and kills the destructive germs of doubt. The doubter knows no true belief. He always belies himself. Either he acts the atheist, the superior free-thinker, while hidden away in a corner of his innermost soul he believes, and has erected an altar before which he secretly offers his prayers; or he may act the believer whilst inwardly deriding his belief, and scorning to-day what he held sacred yesterday, and what he formerly venerated.

All neurotics are really in their souls deeply religious people. Just as their heart continually longs for the spring of their childhood, so they long for the sweet, happy and firm childhood beliefs. It is curious to watch how strangely distorted and in what grotesque disguises this belief returns. For example, they are free of every form of belief, and yet cling to some superstition which only represents a belief in a disguised form. They are afraid to sit down thirteen to a meal; they do not start any important business on Monday; they take it as a good omen when they meet a chimney-sweep; they are unhappy when they meet an old woman in the morning, and so on. They are afraid of the "evil eye," of a curse and of disparagement. They have dethroned the high gods in order to do homage to ridiculous idols. They want to believe, even although it were only belief in their unbelief. Such a metamorphosis of belief is offered to the apparent unbeliever by spiritualism, mysticism, monism and other movements of the time, which all serve one purpose, to satisfy our tremendous need for a belief. For in one corner of the soul there lurks the fear of the Devil. Life has lost all value for those who have *nothing* in which they can believe. Therefore the neurotic creates for himself some sort of substitute belief, in order to say to himself: "There are still some things in which I do firmly believe. I do not doubt everything."

Doubt shows itself in many different ways. In some people it appears to be so harmless, I might almost say so amiable, that it is hardly realized as pathological. One imagines that he has left the door open when leaving his house, and he has to go back just to see if this is really so. Another thinks he has forgotten to turn off the gas. A third doubts whether he has put a stamp on his letter, or even whether he has not forgotten to write the address on the envelope. A fourth wonders whether he has locked up the safe, and other such trifles. All these cases deal with a simple form of doubt, which we consciously excuse by calling it absent-mindedness, carelessness, and exaggerated precaution; all people feel the need to ascribe to their weaknesses some foundation in reason. They need a logical drapery for their illogical affects and actions. In other cases doubt becomes more apparent. A lady wanted to have a dress made, and could not decide whether she should choose a green or a blue material, whether she should go to this or that dressmaker, or whether she should choose this or that fashion. This condition may become so unsatisfactory that the afflicted person cannot come to a decision without an appeal to a higher court. A friend, or the mother, has then to say the decisive word, and dispel the doubt. Such conditions can become extremely painful, and deprive the poor doubter of all joy in life, so that the sufferer fears to make any decisions, and avoids them most carefully. But that is not always the case.

With unconscious malice towards his own Ego, the true doubter seeks out just those situations where his doubt can have free reign. I know a man who always falls in love with two women at the same time, and then faces the question, "Which one shall I marry?" and who cannot come to a decision till he has given them both up. If he asks a friend for his advice, and this friend expatiates on the virtues of Miss A., he is ready to expose her shortcomings, and thus particularly emphasize the virtues and good qualities of Miss B. If he finds the oracle to be favourable to Miss B., he begins the same game with Miss A. And all through life he is always seeking similar situations. Should we call this the spitefulness of Fate, or the ruling of Destiny? He will always be able to find such situations. He receives two excellent offers at the same time, when he is looking out for a change of post, and he does not know which to decide upon; he vacillates for months between two plans for travel, one for going to Norway, and the other to Italy. His entire mode of living is controlled by doubt, and there is no phase of his existence which is not influenced by it. As I have said before, a real doubter doubts everything. He doubts the faithfulness of women, the kindness of human beings, the sincerity of feelings in general, and finally also his own doubt.

I suggested to begin with, that this doubt springs from inner sources. The doubter really doubts himself. His nature is not evenly balanced. A deep cleft divides his soul, which consists, one might say, of two psychic criteria, of which the one says "Yes" and the other "No." His is a split personality, and he has every reason to mistrust himself. Obviously he doubts himself, and he knows that he dare not have confidence in himself. Perhaps I can show this best by a little example: A medical student makes the acquaintance of a young lady at a social gathering; he likes her, and they decide to correspond with each other. They become more intimate through the correspondence; they have secret meetings, and eventually he confesses his love for her. Our student is a doubter, and only a few minutes after his confession the thought comes into his mind: "Do you really love her?" Love is just that which demands a strong, firm, unswerving belief. Yes, perhaps love is nothing else than the firm belief in another person. Where doubt begins, love ends. Let us return to our student. After a week of serious soul searching, he decides to break with the girl, and to explain to her that, owing to his pathological disposition, he cannot think of a serious lasting relationship which will govern his whole future life. He writes the letter, and he has scarcely sent it off when new doubts beset him. Has he expressed himself properly? Could the girl perhaps read the opposite meaning into his letter? Perhaps take it as a confession of his love and a concealed wooing?

And then suddenly a thought comes to him, from which henceforth he cannot free himself, and which develops into a torturing "obsession": If the girl should hold the paper up towards the light, perhaps the letters of both sides might overlap in such a way that this message of refusal might read as a love-letter.

There could be no example more calculated to enable us to comprehend the psychic mechanism of such an obsession. In this young man there are two opposing impulses. One urges: "Take the girl, you are well suited, and she will make you happy." The other warns: "Do not tie yourself to this girl, for who knows if you may not find a better one? Who knows if there may not be a more beautiful one destined for you? Who knows whether you will make her happy?" Two wishes fought in his breast, and both wanted to share in his letter. His doubt and his obsession were therefore justified. The girl must have been able to trace in this farewell letter an indication of his wish not to lose her. His fear lest the letter might also betray the voice of the second psychic factor finds its expression in the doubt whether he has composed the letter rightly. The obsession also which persecuted him for days, that the letter might, when held towards the light, represent a love-letter, was only the expression of the actual thought, perhaps this breaking off is too "transparent" and the girl "sees through" you, and will perceive that you love her, and that the affair is by no means over. The man was overwhelmed by doubts which appeared in the shape of many different questions; which, however, could all be traced back to the basic theme: "Can I? May I? Shall I?" All doubters torment themselves by these questions, and finally they need a second person to make the decision for them, that means they long for an external Imperative. If they do not find this second person, then the so-called compulsion ideas arise; that is to say, they fix their doubt and their everlasting questioning by a compulsion. For every compulsion is a command, an inexorable Thou Must! For example, an end is made of the questioning: "Can I, or may I, go too far?" by the secret Imperative "You can go only thus far, and no farther." There are neurotics who literally can only go a certain limited distance from their house. As long as they move within this radius they are free from anxiety and doubt. If they over-step their self-imposed boundaries, then the anxiety which until then had been held in check awakes with unexpected violence.

Thus doubt and anxiety show the most intimate relationship. They are always found together and can never be quite separated. That man who doubts himself is afraid of himself, and he is also afraid of the demands of life. He who believes in himself feels himself fit for the battle of existence.

On what foundations are these frightful demons of culture based? I have often been able to prove that they can be traced right back to childhood. Education in the idea of fear is one of the characteristic pedagogic crimes of our time. And education making for doubt seems to me to be just as harmful. It is beyond the province of these articles to explain in what a subtle manner the children are robbed of the feeling of independence, and in what dangerous ways one trains them to obey external Imperatives. Doubt and anxiety begin in childhood. The art of education consists in the training of human beings to have neither doubt nor fear, to be people with backbone and far-seeing eyes.

And yet, without the existence of doubt, how could culture have arisen? Fear and doubt are two important levers in the structure of progress. We could not imagine a world devoid of fear and doubt. All progress is based on doubt, and everything in life has a good side and a bad side. That which one man suffers, and which means for him the consuming torture of his existence, forms a part of the force which benefits humanity and advances the great work of progress. Many a doubter is a benefactor to humanity nailed on the cross of neurosis, and treads in his deep suffering those paths which will lead others to salvation.

CHAPTER VII

PSYCHIC OPIUM

Those who have smoked opium, speak enthusiastically of the wonderful pictures which floated before their eyes. The body becomes light as air, the mind becomes so unusually active as to be able to leap all controlling barriers. The excited imagination conjures up alluring pictures of matchless beauty and dazzling splendour before the intoxicated eyes of the smoker. Hasheesh-smokers tell of similar marvels. We can almost understand the mastery of the opium-passion over the individual and his permanent enslavement to it. Of what value to the opium-smoker is this poor world, with its miserable enjoyments, when, with a few inhalations, the gates of paradise open to him? Beautiful dreams are naturally of more value to us than is ugly reality.

There are, as Freud has clearly shown, two kinds of psychic activity: firstly the "pleasure-principle," such as dominates children, animals and savages, forcing them to seek satisfaction by the shortest cut and without hindrance; secondly the "reality-principle," which pre-supposes a complicated psychic machinery, and, while reckoning with realities and hindrances, is prepared to forgo pleasure for the sake of an idea. Opium dreams are dominated solely by the pleasure-principle. The imagination wanders down flowery paths, where only pleasure is to be found. In life, however, we must act according to the reality-principle. I say expressly act and not think, for the pleasure-principle refuses to be suppressed; and the amusement columns of every newspaper testify to the high value which humanity places on pleasure. As a matter of fact, we only live for rare moments of pleasure, and reality is very chary in its distribution of pleasure. Life consists of work, duty, renunciation, and those very rare moments of pleasure.

Now there are people who do not wish to renounce all pleasure; these are the day-dreamers who have the gift of living with open eyes in another self-created world. In that world, the pleasure-principle reigns supreme. In imagination's fantasies, all the foolish wishes which are denied by the ruthlessness and cruelty of life, are fulfilled. The boundless ambition of the neurotic celebrates its resurrection in such day-dreams. The day-dreamers become kings, or at least immeasurably rich. Their fantasies, however, always take such a form as to include some concession to the reality-principle. Thus Mr. X dreams that he has made a wonderful discovery, which brings him in immense wealth. He then proceeds to put his long-cherished plans into execution. Magnificent castles are to appear on all the loveliest spots of the earth, and each is to be the property of Mr. X. In every castle shall dwell a beautiful maiden, who is, of course, deeply in love with Mr. X and dedicated absolutely to him. When he is weary of her, he packs his trunks and goes off to another castle. Of course he has several motors, his own aeroplane of the very latest type, a Zeppelin, his own special train, etc. Or he is a celebrated poet and experiences the delights of a triumphant success. The public acclaims him rapturously; he is carried through the streets in triumph. All the papers publish long articles about the "new star," and compare him with Schiller and Goethe. His friends are struck dumb with admiration and envy. They would never have expected it of so modest a man! How amazed his immediate circle must be! What will his professors say to it? And, above all, that "dull-witted" critic who returned him his first novel as too immature to be worth printing—how astonished he will be! The publishers will now have to pay a fabulous price for his little novel. . . .

And so it goes on deliriously, until the day-dreamer is suddenly brought back to reality by some little commonplace event. This psychic opium renders the dreamer unfit for life. Whilst a consuming ambition urges a man to restless activity, the dreamer is usually content to sink back into inertia. Such a type is "Oblomow," whom Gontscharow has so delightfully portrayed. What has real life to offer to these day-dreamers? Reality is so poor, and the way to success so wearisome, that they prefer to forgo the pleasure of all work, and visit the "cinema of their souls" when they want to indulge in luxurious pictures. They sit there and look on at the fantasies of their own imagination, and await the miracle which shall bring them the fulfilment they long for. They resemble "Nora," the eternal child, always expecting the wonderful to happen. One might also term this type "Haupttreffer Menschen" (those who confidently expect to draw the great prize in a lottery). They wait for the great prize, and, in thought, generously distribute the money they have won among their poor relations and those they like, revenging themselves on those they dislike by passing them over.

This type of day-dreamers (Haupttreffer Menschen) is easily recognisable; for these people are conscious of their day-dreaming. They know that they are building castles in the air, and yet can easily adapt themselves to reality.

But there are day-dreamers who have no idea of their dreaming. These are the people who never have time because they always fritter it away. How often I hear the question: "How on earth do you get the time?" I might reply that I never, or rarely, indulge in day-dreams, and that I always work unless I am not actually resting, for which latter need I make ample provision. For the field of the mind also needs rest if it is to yield a rich harvest. The day-dreamer never has time, he is never punctual, and is always too late. He never has any time to spare because he invariably wastes it. Such people are very difficult to get out of bed. They may awake early, with the best of intentions to go to work. Whereupon begins that strange state of dreaming, in which they are half-awake, half-asleep. Their consciousness is divided between looking, with half-closed eyes, upon a tangled confusion, and gazing vacantly into space. In this manner several hours pass by, and it needs the force of compulsion, or an urgent duty (office, lecture, appointment, etc.) to drag them out of their warm bed. Then they complain of a headache, and feel slack and good-for-nothing for some considerable time, until the influence of the psychic opium is dissipated. As a rule they spend an interminable time over their toilet. They are never ready because they are continually dawdling. They spend half an hour in looking for some article, in putting away this or that; they turn hither and thither, dress and undress themselves over and over again, arrange their tie ten times, and are never finished because of the fact that they go on dreaming while they dawdle. All dawdlers are day-dreamers; they only give half their mind to their work.

As children, these dawdlers are the terror and constant worry of their parents and teachers. They are called in the morning, urged to get up and go to their work, and always give the same stereotyped answer: "I am just going to get up!" "I am just going to dress!" "I am just ready!" This "just" usually means an hour or two. The same thing happens at night; they dawdle about for some hours and get to bed very late. They have to arrange some books, finish their toilet, do their hair, brush their teeth, etc. There is no end to it all. Neither exhortations from their parents nor the making of good resolutions and promises are of any avail. The power and attraction of this sweet dreaming is too strong to resist, and they fall a victim over and over again to the enslaving power.

Psychic opium has unfitted them for life, consequently they are social failures. They are always too late. They appear at the theatre during the first act, to the intense annoyance of the punctual. Similarly they burst in at a concert long after it has begun; miss their train and so keep the meals waiting for them. Their dawdling propensities prevent them from being punctual, and by this they express symbolically their contempt for reality. They are more or less at strife with the world, which obviously does not understand them and treats them unjustly. They are hyper-sensitive and suspect insults and humiliations at every turn. Their dreams have had the effect of making their ambition so boundless, and their neurotic megalomania has reached such a pitch that semblance and reality are merged into one, and a dim lustre from the world of dreams illumines their waking life. From the royal purple robes of his fantasy the day-dreamer saves a few scanty pieces in which he may proudly garb himself in waking life. He therefore despises the insignificant events of every-day life, great artists, brilliantly passed examinations, a good marriage, an excellent post; in short, the whole of society. His secret megalomania produces a state of psychic anarchy which drives him to disregard the laws of society. He delights in showing his secret contempt for society, and gains his end through unpunctuality, cutting people in the street, failing to keep appointments, etc. Such people are absent-minded to a degree. While reading a book they notice suddenly that they have lost themselves in their dreams. While listening to music they suddenly become aware of the flight of their imagination. They engage in conversation, and from their answers one becomes aware of the fact that they have not been listening. They manifest in a marked degree the so-called phenomenon of "Vorbeihören" (deaf-hearing). They are mostly very poor scholars. Hence it happens that highly talented children may become very bad scholars and never fulfil their early promise. Teachers complain that the child, though very talented, cannot be attentive. All the resolutions of these children come to nothing because the realities of instruction do not interest them. Only that teacher who plays upon their imagination can captivate them and focus their interest on a particular subject. Otherwise, day-dreams are liable to thrust themselves forward into the dry stuff, and that is the end to all resolutions, to the last remaining bit of attention and the will to study.

I have no doubt whatever that this tendency to day-dreams is steadily on the increase at the present time. The poorer our life is in rich and stirring experiences, the further are we enticed into the labyrinth of our dreams. We must not leave out of account the harmful tendency of modern education, which acts entirely on the pleasure-principle. Children are spoilt, praised, petted and altogether made too much of. Every one wants his child to become great, famous, far above the average. When these ambitious hopes are cruelly shattered by reality, the disappointed person falls back on his day-dreams, in which there are no disappointments, no hampering limitations. Children should, therefore, be educated more for reality; they should be taught to see life as it is, to be prepared for the struggle of existence. They should be taught modesty betimes, and the realization of our own insignificance in comparison with the general average.

It seems to me that music, when indulged in to excess, is especially calculated to foster the growth of day-dreams. A drama forces our thoughts into a particular channel, compels us to follow a given train of thought, as in the case of a novel, or other forms of literature. But in the case of music, each one can think and feel what he pleases. Music stimulates the emotions at the expense of the intellect. I have found the best examples of day-dreamers among music lovers. In the case of Wagnerites especially, this dream state attains a pitch of ecstasy worthy of a detailed description. I shall refer to this subject again later on. I myself am a great lover of music and an enthusiastic musician. But excess of any kind seems to me harmful. Nowadays every child plays, whether it has talent or not, and is dragged to concerts at an early age. Children with tendencies to day-dreaming (such as I have described as dawdlers) should only be allowed to take up music if they show great talent. It is just among the highly gifted musicians that many day-dreamers are to be found. They weave their fantasies into their playing and into their compositions. They dream with open eyes, but in the language of music. Yes, if only the notes could speak, we should be able to interpret strange dreams, and conflicts between pleasure and reality would be revealed to us, whereby we might obtain a better understanding of life. Music also is a psychic opium, which, if indulged in to excess, can harm us and unfit us for life. If we could but understand the secret language! If! . . .

But very few people divulge their day-dreams. Once put into words, their magic is destroyed. The door which leads to the magic garden of day-dreams is carefully guarded. The uninitiated may not enter there. His clumsy foot might tread on the delicate flowers, whose poisonous odour is so sweetly benumbing, and helps us to forget the pains which brutal reality has caused us. In this labyrinth grow the red poppies which contain the psychic opium. The secret of all pleasure is intoxication. We seek it in love, in alcohol, in enthusiasm, and in day-dreams. Intoxication means forgetting the world. So sad is life for most people that forgetting implies happiness! One of the greatest advantages of culture is that it teaches us to extract pleasure out of actual life. A fine poem, the dying strains of a beautiful song, an interesting landscape, an engrossing novel, an animated conversation, a successful enterprise, a duty fulfilled, a charitable deed, these are realities which can bring us great pleasure, and yet whose relationship with the airy realm of our imagination cannot be denied. Finally, all life is a compromise.

Only he who knows how to combine the pleasure-principle and the reality-principle can be happy. His dreams are full of realities, and reality has the effect of a dream fulfilled.

CHAPTER VIII

POENA TALIONIS

Not even the most fleeting of impressions can be lost. What man has collected in the course of years that he bequeaths to his descendants. Instinct is the memory and the experience of the unconscious. This law applies not only to humanity at large but also to every individual. Humanity possesses a secret memory of all past events and impressions. This is how it comes about that powers which in reality belong to the past remain active in the consciousness of people. This fact can be proved by innumerable examples in Crowd Psychology. We will speak of only one of them now—of a law which was valid once; later, was replaced by other laws, but nevertheless remains to-day still in force.

In Roman Law there existed a law of retaliation which was called the "Poena Talionis." If a person had sworn falsely, his right hand was cut off; this also happened to the thief who had laid his hand on other people's property. If a case of blackmail required a severe punishment, then the tongue was torn out. Even the old Germans were governed by this principle of retaliation. We can also find in the Bible some passages which bear on this: thus, "An eye for an eye, and a tooth for a tooth." Or "With what measure ye measure, shall it be meted out to you again." Jus talionis has never disappeared from the crowd consciousness. To pay back in equal coin is a universal law. The lofty endeavours of Christian religion to leave revenge to heaven have unfortunately met with very little success. Vengeance is still something personal—very often only too personal.

Those who are of opinion that this Jus Talionis is only used against others, are very much mistaken. We often bring upon ourselves punishment which is more relentless and severe than would have been the case if it had been dealt out by others. Now, certain nervous symptoms can be only understood by taking into consideration this law of retaliation, of "Jus Talionis."

I have spoken of nervous symptoms, and I have pointed out the characteristics of these "talionis" phenomena. They only appear in neurotics, and are a sign of a deep consciousness of guilt. How the symptoms have come about, we do not know. They are generally unconscious psychic processes, in which fear of an avenging higher power, Nemesis, eventually develops into anxiety, into a retributive power. The neurotic punishes himself for his supposed sins, and then imagines his punishment is the direct consequence of an avenging Nemesis.

Enough of generalities. Let us observe a typical case of such "Poena Talionis." A married man, strictly religious, had his right hand paralysed for some years. The anaesthesia of this hand permitted one to stick needles quite deeply into the flesh without the patient stirring a muscle. The diagnosis was not difficult. It was a case of genuine hysteria, in a form which we generally find only in women. And what was the cause of it? The married man, who did not wish, even in thought, to break the Sixth Commandment, had taken a country house just before his illness. He had arrived late in the evening. In the morning he went into the garden to walk round. The proprietress of the country house, a beautiful young woman, met him, bade him welcome and shook hands with him. On the impulse of the moment he took her hand, pressed it warmly, thanked her for her greeting and expressed the hope that they might become good neighbours.

The touch of the soft, caressing hand, seemed very

wonderful to him. A hot current had passed from that hand through his arm and over his whole body. His imagination became excited to a fantasy, and his hand burned as if in a glowing fire. He fought with all the strength of his mind and will against the tempting pictures, against the sin. And he fought successfully. The hand became colder and colder—so cold that it lost its feeling entirely. The "Poena Talionis" had been fulfilled. God had punished him in the part where he had sinned. In addition, the arm which he had raised in greeting became half paralysed. Co-incident with these symptoms, another strange thing occurred. He forgot the proprietress and all about the whole affair entirely. It was cut right out of his consciousness. He had committed no sin. Everything was buried in the obscurity of his unconscious mind, for he had atoned for it and punished himself severely. He was the wrong-doer, the accuser, and the judge, in one and the same person. And perhaps he was more severe than God would have been.

Another example shows us the Jus Talionis in an ethical conflict without the intermixture of religious principles. A lady of about forty years of age gradually began to stop taking food. Her meals became smaller and smaller day by day. First she gave up meat, and then sweets. Later she gave up all solid food, until finally she could only take soup.

This lady had lost her father, whom she had loved above everything—a father whom she had repeatedly offended. After his death remorse began to appear. Everything she had done against the will of her father came before her with cruel clearness. She remembered the first scenes of disobedience in her childhood. It was at the mid-day meal, when she did not want to take any soup. Her father made a great point of it. He contended that the soup was nourishing, and more important than any other course. In vain; the obstinate child followed the example of the boy in " Shockheaded Peter "—" I will not eat my soup, No! No!—I shall not eat my soup to-day!"

Now, after so many years, and after the death of her father, she realized the wickedness of her obstinacy. At last she had become obedient.

Do not let us imagine that it is only the living who have power over us. Often it is the dead who are the greatest, the hardest tyrants. The living person can be moved. The dead remains silent and immovable. So much of what we do is only belated obedience. Thus our patient punished herself for all that she had done in opposition to the spirit of her father by a belated, slavish obedience. She placed herself under Poena Talionis and went to the other extreme of what she had done in her youth. Now she could eat nothing but soup.

Of course this punishment would not have been in accordance with her father's wishes. He would certainly have brushed away the cobwebs of non-existent sins had he been alive. As it is in real life, so it is in neurosis. One uses the letter of the law, but how often one misses the spirit. Thus the father would have protested against the use of this punishment in his name and would have exercised his prerogative of mercy. Now that he is dead, this prerogative is in the power of another authority who soothes all pain and ends all suffering—Time.

Every person possesses in himself his greatest enemy, and at the same time his greatest friend—his own Ego.

However he may ridicule and scorn the idea, conscience never lets him out of its grip. And when he thinks himself to be most free and independent—in a moment he feels the sharp claws at his throat, and must writhe with pain, sink to the ground, and bend the knee before that enigmatic power which drives us through the obscure paths of life towards a distant unknown goal.

Ibsen is right when he demands for the man of action a " robust " conscience. All neurotics suffer from too sensitive a conscience.

" Nothing is wrong with me," once said to me a lady who was suffering from agoraphobia, " except the lack of a little light-heartedness. Put a little light blood into my veins and I shall be quite well." How striking! How true! How candid!

But had she offered me all the treasures in the world, I could not have procured that light-heartedness for her. It will never appear where it does not already exist. Her agoraphobia was a "Poena Talionis." She reproached herself for having " gone too far " on one occasion. Now she punished herself and left the house no more. Whenever she was required to go anywhere she always made the same excuse: " It is so far; it seems to me such an immense distance."

A further punishment she visited upon her husband. He had jealously watched her when she was a young woman, and had forbidden her to go out alone. Now she felt she dared not be left alone at all, and would not allow him away from her side for a moment. If she actually went out on occasion, she was obliged to take quite an escort with her. Thus she punished not only herself, but those around her had to participate in the punishment.

Countless obscure complaints are really only "Poena Talionis." A girl suffers from severe and apparently incurable headaches. All remedies, whether internal or external, seem powerless to alleviate her terrible sufferings, which are hysterical in nature.

She once untruthfully pleaded a headache to her mother in order that she might stay at home. This event was the the first link in a chain of incidents about which she severely reproached herself. At that time her head was turned by a cousin. Why had she lied to her mother that evening? What anxiety her poor little mother had shown then. Now the pains stabbed and bored through her head as though they would say—If only you hadn't done that then; if only you had told your mother all about it!

I often ask myself, what is the use of all the laws and penalties? Why all this complicated paraphernalia of judges, prosecutors and defendants? Those who fall under the law are not those whose punishment is the most severe. They are mostly criminals, having the before mentioned "robust" conscience, to whom punishment is no more than unpleasant, and only more or less of a hindrance.

"Justitia" seems to me like a scarecrow, set up to prevent hungry sparrows from damaging the cornfield. It frightens only the timid inexperienced birds; the cheeky variety have long known how to treat a scarecrow, and even how to avoid a living watcher.

But what are all the anguish and penalties of public justice, in comparison with the limitless flood of sorrow and remorse which wells up from the soul of the penitent? Every moment his trembling hand plunges the cold steel of reproach into his own quivering flesh. No second passes without thousands feeling it their duty to repent of sins which either they have never committed or which are not sins at all.

Thus humanity purchases its progress at the price of endless sacrifices. We move towards a proud time when there will be no other judge on earth than that in one's own breast, no other shame than shame of oneself, no other punishment than "Poena Talionis" which one dictates oneself.

CHAPTER IX

THE FEAR OF JOY

MANY years ago I saw a very attractive theatrical play in which a son, who was believed to have been dead, was expected home. Every one trembled with fear of the effect upon the aged, weak mother. How could one best break to her the joyful news, as she had not even yet heard of the miracle? Was it not possible that the extraordinary excitement caused by the unexpected event might bring about her sudden death? Eventually, however, all ended well, and the author came to the comforting conclusion that joy cannot kill. All that fear of joy, of too great joy, was superfluous.

To me the problem then seemed a little absurd. How can one possibly conceive the thought of being afraid of joy? Do not all people seek joy, and hunt for it all their life long, by lawful and unlawful ways?

It was only after many years that I recognized that the poet had, in this question, dealt with an important problem of the time although in an extreme example. A wise German saga tells us of Till Eulenspiegel, who, coming down a hill, showed an unhappy face, and was angry because he had to think of the next ascent. There are more such Eulenspiegels abroad in the world than one might imagine. It is considered exceptionally wise not to feel too much joy about happiness, lest one should provoke misfortune. "After laughter follows weeping." So we were told as children. In the schoolroom one learns several uplifting quotations and little stories to prove this rule. "Happiness and glass, how easily they both break!" "Happiness and unhappiness, how rarely either comes alone!" And lastly, the very wise saying of Solomon: "No man is to be accounted happy before his death," has been held up as the very height of wisdom.

How is it possible then to enjoy one's happiness? "After joy follows sorrow," says the proverb. Even poets teach us restraint in joy. I am especially thinking of the poem by Schiller called: *Der Ring des Polycrates*, where in the face of exceptionally good luck the guest turns away "with horror." Thus we have learnt to fear happiness and too great a joy.

Of what use against these exhortations in one's

youth are the good teachings of Horace who has expressed himself by the splendid *Carpe diem,* so well translated into German by Baumbach as *Heut ist heut!* (To-day is to-day.) There has always remained a bitter sediment in every joy, a secret fear that "the gods wished to destroy us," that happiness would be followed by misfortune, and that the contrast would make the inevitable misfortune appear all the greater. Is this the right form of teaching? Happiness should not make us reckless; but should our happiness be poisoned by the thought of its inevitable end?

One thing seems certain to me. The so-called "Weltschmerz" may arise because we have banned nearly all "Joy in Life" from our lives. We have some joys, small, timid, little joys, but the real, great, wonderful "Joy in Life" will soon be a thing of the past. How few people answer the conventional question, "How do you do?" with the truthful, honest answer: "Thank you, excellently!" with sparkling eyes and their whole being emanating satisfaction. How rarely one finds these happy beings. Most of them will have some complaint to make about their health, about their business, about their family, or those in authority over them, or the political conditions, and so on. The whole mood of humanity seems to me to be, to a large extent, transposed into the minor key.

Was there ever a time when one heard of so many suicides of young people? How pitiful this Youth, which at the first disappointment throws away life like a valueless rag! Unfortunately it is the real joy of life which is lacking.

One can observe without much difficulty the life-weariness, as well as the fear of joy, in modern tendencies of the time. Even Science herself can be affected only too easily by this tendency and attires herself in the latest fashion. Nowadays she wears a little ascetic mantle, which is so much too short for her that it is unable quite to cover up her bad conscience. Out of its folds there peep Superstition and its father, Belief. Savonarolas do not die out. The gloomy spirit of the Middle Ages still wanders through our modern streets, calling "Woe! woe! woe!" over sinning humanity. Repent and renounce, that your life may be long. If you desire a long life, you must not shorten it by indulgence and joy! Always give careful consideration as to what is healthy and what is harmful. Renounce! Renounce! Renounce! Avoid that which poisons the soul, and beware of stimulants of all kinds. Stimulants are sins against the Holy Ghost of Hygiene.

There is no doubt that this ascetism is in keeping with the Spirit of the Time. But the Spirit of the Time is only the sum total of the minds of individuals. Only the knowledge of the psychology of the individual can give us an understanding of the psychology of the crowd.

The study of neurotics will be most valuable for this investigation, because neurosis shows us general phenomenon caricatured by magnification, or embellished by diminution. And it is the magnification which most clearly shows us the general faults which otherwise might have escaped unnoticed.

Amongst neurotics we find a whole group where fear of joy plays an important part. There are those unfortunates who are afraid of every joy, because they maintain that in their experience bad times invariably follow. As soon as a feeling of joy in life becomes apparent, they feel uncomfortable and become possessed by a slight, but ever-increasing feeling of anxiety: Do not rejoice too much, things will soon go badly for you! This is the beginning of a very wide-spread disease, which later on assumes quite grotesque forms. These patients evolve an ingenious system by which they deprive themselves of all joys in life, and which induces them to do exactly the opposite things to those which would give them joy. They plunge into all those present-day movements which demand self-control and renunciation. They become enthusiastic disciples of the different abstinence movements. They leave off drinking and smoking. They become vegetarians, and gulp down huge quantities of badly prepared vegetables in defiance of possibly fatal results, while they are consumed with longing for a savoury roast. They deny themselves love, and that which is sometimes greater—success. In fact, they do just those things which are in reality unpleasing to them. They do not marry the girl they love, but another, who becomes to them a real "punishment of God." They study scientific works, although the reading of them is a torture (to read a novel is a deadly sin!). They struggle with difficult music (an alluring waltz is as much taboo as the exciting novel!), and in the end they succeed in transforming all the joys of this world into Work and Duty.

Why do they act thus? What inner necessity forces them to it? Such a powerful psychic impulse cannot evolve of itself without some compelling motive! Every creature longs for joy and enjoyment! Man cannot be born only to suffer, however often we are told that this is so!

If we inquire further of these strange sufferers,

they are either silent, or we get at last a hesitating answer. They hear an inner voice which tells them: "You are not deserving. You are much too wicked for that." In other words: they have a "bad conscience," and think that they do not deserve the joys of life. They subdue their joy, and bad conscience acts as a mute. They are their own accusers and their own judges!

I know an actor who might have become famous. In spite of a great talent, which showed infinite possibilities, he was never able to get away from himself and to express the whole of his power and his art. Before a performance he would say to himself: "Of course they will laugh at you, and you will fail miserably. You don't deserve anything else. You are a bad lot, and you cannot possibly get on." In this mood he goes on the stage, and has to fight continually against his hindering and disturbing inner self. And through all his joys he hears the dreadful comment: "You do not deserve it." He kisses a sweet girl, after having been consumed with longing for her. As she sinks unresistingly into his arms, he hears the veto, "You do not deserve it," and he tears himself, under some pretext or other, from her surrendering embrace. He loses his finest engagements, and offends his best friends. He does not deserve their love.

What happens with this man in full consciousness, may remain in the case of others below the threshold of consciousness, and yet may decide their fate. Many a hand which might well reach for the highest goal stops and hesitates, as if thinking it over once more. A silent humility forces them to renunciation and self-denial. A sad vein of resignation runs through all the actions of these people. Their success seems to them unmerited, and they feel almost ashamed of it. This silent form of "Fear of Joy" explains many actions which would otherwise be inexplicable. A man has been secretly wooing a girl for a long time. Every one waits for him to say the final word, and to propose marriage to her. Months and years pass, and at length the first wooer watches, with mournful resignation, how another obtains the happiness he had so ardently desired. Those men are of the same type who feel themselves uplifted when a woman accepts their wooing. She, so high, so beautiful, she, the goddess, has favoured him, a poor mortal. He does not deserve that. He shrinks from such happiness, till time effaces the picture of the goddess slowly, but surely, with a cruel hand, and replaces it with that of a human being with all its faults and virtues. There are also those who dream of long voyages, and who devour all literature descriptive of travel. They study all the guide-books, and live in their imagination in Italy, in Norway; cross the ocean in modern giant vessels, and yet, in spite of all their plans for travel, they remain at home; they find, as one always can, some trifling pretext. To tell the truth, it is because they wish to deny themselves their greatest happiness. They are afraid of too great a joy. Gloomy and superstitious forebodings penetrate into their souls, especially in the twilight at the end of the day. The air resounds with secret warnings: "Don't do it; you will have to suffer for it!" "Every joy is paid for with pain." And the little anxious heart shrinks back and renounces the fulfilment of its longing. How many such longing thoughts have already been sacrificed to this fear of joy! Every second some wish sinks unfulfilled and soulless to the ground, because fear of joy has transformed joy into fear. And behind this fear is hidden that scourge of our time—Conscience. We all have a very sensitive conscience, and all renunciations are more or less severe punishments arbitrarily meted out by the "Inner Judge." Nietzsche, by an exhaustive investigation, has exposed the social roots of this conscience. One may easily make the error of holding religion responsible for conscience. It seems more probable to me that the bad conscience of humanity has created religion. Thus Christianity has been the bad conscience of Judaism, and so has remained till to-day. It would lead us too far afield if we tried to find out the social roots of this highly interesting phenomenon. A different aetiology of conscience seems to me more important and fruitful for presentation just now.

It is characteristic of the education of the cultured person that, with the necessary moral conscience, he is also inoculated with the fear of joy. If one thinks how often children, small and big, are reminded of their wickedness, one cannot wonder that there are people who grow up to think themselves evil and contemptible. A child hears: "You are not worthy that the sun should shine on you!" If the child, as a grown up neurotic, shows an inexplicable fear of the sun, and can walk only in the shade without a feeling of anxiety, then this phobia, besides other origins, may also have this as one of its causes. *Die Sonne bringt es an den Tag.* (The sun will bring it to light.) Another child is continually being told of the benefits which his parents shower upon him, and at the same time is constantly having pointed out to him what an unrepentant, unnatural and ungrateful creature he is. The parents set themselves up as models of virtue, just as if they had not themselves committed exactly the same misdeeds in their youth. The consequence is that people are inclined to think that others are better and nobler than they are themselves. All suppressed impulses and hungry instincts which exist in us, and which come up in obscure and indistinct dreamlike wishes and repressed longings, are counted unclean and wicked. This creates a feeling of inferiority in comparison with other people. There are far too many lies in this world of ours.

These are only a few observations on this important problem, which is known as the Fear of Joy. Not our children only but all people should be educated up to the joy of life. Could we not banish the sinister spirit of asceticism and bring up humanity to a noble enjoyment of life? I do not want to be misunderstood. I am not an apostle of egoistic joy of life at any price, without any consideration. Joy in beautiful and good things is one of the most uplifting joys in this world. We must bring up children to rejoice in good and beautiful things, but not through fear of retribution and punishment of hell. We must love Goodness because it is good, and because we wish to represent a higher type of man. It should be our endeavour to educate ourselves to be Noble-Men. To rejoice, means also to rejoice with others, means to give joy to others through one's own joy.

The world is longing for emancipating laughter. Merry, cheerful Pan is dead; and in this strenuous period of so much machinery we seek in vain for his traces.

But I notice that I have begun to preach. I preach the new religion of Joy of Life. And would this be such a bad thing? I imagine a time (which will never come) with temples of joy, and with people who are capable of accepting life as Joy. Here the psychologist becomes a Utopian. Are we ripe for such a religion? Perhaps a few chosen ones among us. What would this world be without a strong belief to form the basis of our social order, and to secure order and morality?

Every period needs its religion. It makes the problem of the Intellectuals immensely difficult that we have only the religion of the past at our disposal. All founders of religion bring us a religion for the future. The present is always left out.

Let us descend from the heights of philosophical enlightenment to everyday life. A beautiful old song continually rings in my ears. Why does one never hear it now in merry circles? Why do people sing so little? Imagine the modern " At Home " day, and the lady of the house starting the song: " Enjoy life while the lamp is still burning, and gather the rose before it withers."

CHAPTER X

WE AND OUR MONEY

The normal person would not think it possible that there are people who are unable to adapt themselves in any way whatever to the use of money. They never learn how to deal with money or how rightly to value it. All financial transactions are a difficult problem to them, which they prefer to shun. To these people the payment of a debt is a great task, and the demanding of money an impossibility. They tremble all over whenever they have to make any decision in money matters, and they become the victims of charlatans of various kinds, not from stupidity, but from their inability rightly to grasp the responsibilities and values of money. But let us leave these extreme cases, which we will go into later. Does not even the so-called normal person act strangely with regard to money? There are hardly two people who behave alike in a monetary transaction.

Already in children, one can observe immense differences in their valuation of money. Some children have from early childhood a keen sense of the value of money. They are happy when it is given to them, they collect it and save it, play with it, are proud of their treasure, show it to every one, talk continually about it, and ask and beg for "tips" from their real, or so-called, uncles and aunts. They know well the meaning of "much" or "little," are generally quick at reckoning, and already as children are accustomed to all sorts of monetary and business transactions. They sell and exchange stamps, exchange pens for books, and will even do another's home-work for a good price.

Those are born business men, dealers, whose whole life becomes a struggle for money, who view everything from a monetary standpoint, Time, Love, Fatherland, Art.

Other children show an entire lack of appreciation of money. In one of Dickens's novels, a little boy asks his father what money is. The father is very puzzled. Money is difficult to define; money is money, at last he replies, money is money. To these children, however, money is not money. They are embarrassed when some one gives them money. What should they do with it? If they are rich children, whose every wish is fulfilled, or who are not allowed to buy anything themselves, they smile dutifully and gratefully when they are promised that the money shall be put in a money-box and kept for them. What do they care about the future? And many of them know that Father has lots of money, and that some day his money will to some extent belong to them. Others are afraid to take money in their hand, as if it would burn and injure them. Or as if it were dirty, and the touch of it would cause stains and illness. At the same time they look at the treasure with secret longing. They are ashamed to betray their greed for it.

Even grown-ups show this shame. Every one likes to play the part of the idealist who does not care about money.

Very few people admit openly that they love money, want it, and wish to acquire it. Indeed there are many professions in which it is dangerous to disclose this craving for money. The reputation of a business man generally depends on the cleverness with which he hides his profit. The doctor must never disclose that he also is dependent upon the acquisition of money. He must accept his fee with hesitation and apparent unwillingness, as if forced to do so by necessity, rather than obeying his own impulses, and must express in his face that he would prefer to do without it altogether. This is in accordance with the expectation of people, especially in German countries; but in other countries a more straightforward attitude is taken in this respect.

All of us have a hidden fear, which is the motive for strange behaviour on our part; we are afraid of being taken advantage of and of being exploited by others. We therefore prefer to have dealings with our friends, acquaintances, or such people as have been well recommended to us.

We shall be no less taken advantage of—because the whole of life consists in one taking advantage of another, and all are deceived deceivers—but we save ourselves anxiety and the trouble of taking precautions, and from the after doubt as to whether we have received our due or not. We are always on guard against the badness of the world. There are so many bad people in the world—is an old saying. No wonder. Because money matters have a bad effect upon nearly every one. Money arouses the most brutal instincts in mankind. Envy, avarice, tyranny, greed of gain and profit, are wild creatures to have power over us, and very difficult to tame by moral and educational means. We are suspicious of other people, only because we understand ourselves and can see our own depths. Only good people are trustful of others.

This gives us an insight into the origin of the different attitudes of people towards money. Blood-thirsty, sinister thoughts are connected with money. Money poisons human relationships. The tragedy of " The Rheingold " is the tragedy of everyday life.

There is a remarkable phenomenon of the psychic life which is especially revealed in dreams. We discover a series of " Symbolic Equations " as I have called this phenomenon. One of these equations suggests to us that money may be symbolic of dirt, excreta, blood, air, time, and life. Even the old books on dream interpretation show this. If one walked along a muddy country road, the dream interpreter prognosticated great riches—wallowing in money.

We call a usurer a blood-sucker. Money symbolizes air, because a merchant " erstickt " * if he is unable to pay up all his debts by the end of the time limit. A miser is called a " dirty " rascal, and in everyday language money stands for filth (filthy lucre). We also find further from the observation of dreams, that people dream very frequently about numbers

* Austrian expression=suffocates.

and money. These numbers often have a very important significance as I have shown in *Die Sprache des Traumes* (Verlag Von J. F. Bergmann, Wiesbaden, 1911). They signify a guilty conscience. In analysing these dreams, one is astonished to find what an excellent mathematician the unconscious mind of man is.

The numbers show a marvellous connexion with certain dates of deaths, births, and of important and fateful dates in one's own life, and so on. These dates may have been entirely forgotten by one's conscious mind, but have been stored up in the unconscious. There is really no forgetting an impression. Every experience produces an everlasting impression, and the so-called forgetting is only a submergence into subterranean depths, which are, however, always accessible to dream. Dream, like a bold diver, brings up these apparently forgotten memories into the dim obscurity of sleep.

But what a strangely different aspect we get of a person after the exposure of his suppressed emotions. We are all very much alike, and this truth cannot be sufficiently often repeated. The line of demarcation between good and bad is very slight. We are all very miserly; but in what very different ways does this avarice show itself. The fundamental and universal egoistic instinct for money, which is in reality only a disguised form of craving for power, has undergone many transformations. One person is mean with money, another with love, a third with life, and a fourth with memories. We all have our secret money-boxes where we store up our treasures. From time to time we steal up into the dim garrets of our souls, and anxiously and with beating hearts (lest we should be discovered) count over our wealth.

Our relations towards money demand a tranquil and firm attitude of mind. The child who can handle money well has a calm conscience, which gives promise of a strong conscience later on. We should not ponder deeply about money, but should accept it lightly and pass it on. We should acquire and redistribute it, without reflecting upon how much trouble, sweat, blood and worry is attached to it.

The neurotic has lost this unbiassed attitude towards money. His lust for the glittering gold has been too strong. The curse of the Rhein-gold pursues him through his whole life, and the forms which this curse takes are very strange.

One person is afraid to handle money, because it might contain germs of disease. He disinfects the coins, and the paper money he places in protecting envelopes.

Another cannot keep money; it runs away like water through his hands. This is a neurosis from which the heirs of rich men frequently suffer, thus showing their unconscious contempt for wealth, and masking the unsatisfied greed which they once felt for their father's or mother's money. Money, then, only becomes of real value to them when they acquire it for themselves; but that of their parents "never gets warm in their hands." They long for any opportunity to spend it. They naturally fall an easy prey, but this is only in accordance with their desires; they are powerless to refuse any request for money, especially from the poor. This type is well-known to the professional beggars who swarm in our great cities, and who make a comfortable living out of the generosity of those people who cannot handle money. They know their victims quite well, and only pass on their addresses to their best friends and brothers in the profession, who in return have to hand over a proportion of their spoils. All sorts of pathetic stories are poured out; mothers die, distraint or imprisonment threatens, a girl's honour is at stake, a provision has to be made for a widow, fees for a poor student's exams have to be found, and so on. And their moneyed victim gives with both hands, as if he would make atonement for the sins of his father as well as for his own.

There is another type which cannot pay a tradesman's bill without being subsequently seized with doubt as to whether they have paid it or not. They return to ask the tradesman: Have I already paid your last bill? The tradesman looks it up in his book—Yes, the bill has been paid on such and such a date. But even this does not satisfy the poor creatures. The doubt returns again, and even the assurance of the tradesman cannot pacify them, because he, being only human, might have made a mistake himself. A deep feeling of guilt expresses itself in this neurosis. For all those who cannot handle money rightly suffer from an excessive consciousness of guilt. In dreams, neurosis, and in life, money frequently signifies guilt. Money is the symbol of guilt. What tortures these people is the inner reproach of a secret debt which they have not yet paid—that is to say of a sin for which they have not atoned. . . .

This burden has not been removed, and so every debt and every bill with which they have to deal becomes a symbol of guilt to them. The guilt may not have been an actual experience at all. The ethical lapses of neurotics are comprised in their thoughts; and are in most cases fantasies and wishes which have gone beyond the permitted bounds, and then, having been recognized by their conscience as criminal, have been repressed.

If an heir hardly has the patience to wait for his father's death, but already pictures to himself what he will do with the money, then he creates with these fantasies a bad conscience, which hinders him from adopting a well-balanced attitude towards money.

Excessive miserliness is also a neurosis. Money is really only a key to power and to possession. To people who suffer from this neurosis the "means" is of more importance than the "end." They suffer this punishment because they want to conquer the world for themselves with their treasures. Money means everything—laziness, love, gormandizing, friendship, society, travelling, works of art. Everything can be got with money, at least an apparent equivalent. The miser sees the possibility of attainment of all these before him, but he postpones the opportunity until he has amassed more wealth. And he must collect more and more. At last his love is entirely possessed by money. Money with him takes the place of friend, art, and travelling. His life is constituted of money equivalents. Now and then one finds an exception: a man who saves for a long time, and then suddenly becomes open-handed, and plays the Grand Seigneur.

Then there is quite a special variety of these people who suffer from a money complex. They are those who have possessions, but are perpetually in dread of becoming poor. What is safe in this world? Nothing counts as safe to them. The bank might fail in the event of war; their own house might collapse (has this not happened in San Fransisco?); their investments in shares might become valueless if war arose. From time to time one reads in the papers of a shortage of money; and one may be sure that these neurotics will have drawn their deposits out of the banks because they had begun to tremble for the safety of their property. They are incessantly haunted by the spectre of poverty, and feel that they are incapable of earning a penny. It is true that they have inherited, but they have never earned. The pleasure that these people feel when they have themselves acquired a small sum is indescribable. They feel that one of the bonds which chains them in the torture chamber of anxiety is loosened.

I could multiply these examples, but these few will suffice. They show us that the rich are not always as happy in their possessions as one generally imagines. The most serious cases of neurosis, I have always found amongst the very rich people. The poor can never become so seriously affected, because they possess a powerful remedy against neurosis—work. Heavy work rarely permits the development of such complicated psychic phenomena. The rich are not to be envied, and it requires great acumen in the education of the children of the rich to turn them into healthy, happy people with a capacity for work.

It is one of the important tasks for parents and teachers to train children in the proper handling of money. Perhaps the best method of doing this is to encourage them to earn it themselves. If each coin and note they have represents the direct result of their own effort, it will follow automatically that they also attach the right value. It is quite a mistake to give children no money at all to handle; because when they are grown up they are helpless in face of the problems of money and acquisition. They can neither spend nor acquire, or do anything else connected with it. Therefore children should learn in good time how to value money, and to value it rightly.

It is a dangerous thing for them, as children at home, to get into the way of over-valuing money. We must not despise money, as it is one of the necessities of life; but we must guard ourselves carefully against over-valuation. We must impress upon the children the fact that money and happiness do not depend upon each other; and that one may earn and yet keep one's ideals. What can be said of those parents who always tell their daughters to catch a rich man, and their sons to make only a wealthy marriage?

All parents long for wealth for their children, because the outward show arouses the envy of those who possess not.

If I could ask of Fate what I would have for my children, I would ask for them a contented mind, the power of adapting themselves to all circumstances of life, and of obtaining from every hour all the happiness it has to offer.

And one thing particularly I would beg of Fate for them, that they should not succumb to the temptation of the Spirit of the Age, to the wild scramble after money, which, one gathers from the example set by the New World, will be the outstanding feature of our Modern Times. Time should not be money, or not *only* money for them; but Time should be love, nature, art, rest, happiness, enjoyment, useful work cheerfully accomplished, good deeds, comfort, relaxation and . . . only then, money.

But we are a long way yet from that ideal age in which it will be said—Time is Happiness.

CHAPTER XI

ENVY

An ugly yellow worm gnaws at our soul, and, with a hundred poisoned fangs, seeks eagerly for prey. If we cut off its head, then a double head will grow in its place, as it was with the Lernaic snake. Its glistening body fills our soul and saps our best energies. It makes us blind and deaf, and holds continually before us the mirror of the greedy Ego, which wishes to see and hear only itself, and to have everything for itself.

Unfortunately we know ourselves only too little. We consider ourselves to be patterns of virtue, but our keen eyes see only the fault of others. It is only when we win through to the knowledge that all beings (with very few exceptions) are alike, and that good and evil dwell in every breast, that we can recognize in the faults of others, our own, and can attain that all-knowing and all-understanding humility which distinguishes the wise man from the fool. But then, by-and-by, we can also acquire a sad insight into the tremendous part played by envy in the individual psychic life and in humanity in general.

It is the nature of Man to be entirely egoistical. He would like to have everything for himself; he is the centre of the world, and everything revolves round his own wishes. The first stirrings of envy are aroused by another's possessions. And how curious is that quality of envy! Even the mere fact that a certain thing is possessed by some one else, causes it to become an object of envy. We can see this demonstrated repeatedly every day. Just divide an apple into two halves. The other person's half will always seem the larger one to us, however equal the division. There is no escape from this optical delusion. I once had an old coat which I could not possibly wear any longer. I gave it to one of my poorer colleagues, for whom this old coat served as his Sunday best. The first time he came to me in his "new" coat, I was astonished at its fine appearance, and could not understand why I had given it away. Thus possession by another had changed my opinion. We realize far too little how possession decreases the value of an object. How often do I console young men in love, who complain to me about their bitter anguish, and who contemplate taking their own lives on account of the hopelessness of their love. I point out to them that they can never possess a person so completely as when they have never possessed him or her at all. The ideal image of their beloved remains indestructible and unsullied in their soul. It stands the test of time, and no power in the world can affect the image. Even time cannot destroy it. Memory transfigures it and enhances its charm. How different is the case when the lovers have obtained their beloved ones, and when they have become their possession. After the first varnish of infatuation has worn off, the stains begin gradually to appear. Their ideal is only a human being after all, although they had believed it to be divine. The qualities of a human being must be there, and however great the virtues may be, there must of necessity exist faults also. Each fault takes a little from their illusion, and finally there remain only a few poor miserable fragments, the last fragments of a proud array, wherewith they had adorned the goddess of their fantasy. Possession is loss.

This is indeed the greatest curse weighing down humanity. Humanity has not the capability of enjoying possession in the present. It appreciates its own possession only when it is surrounded by the envy of others. What ecstasy it gives one to be envied! The whole cruelty of man is exposed in this quality. We should realize how bitter envy is, and how it can gnaw at our innermost souls and make a torture of existence. But we do not realize it, or we do not want to realize it. We fight for success, which should bring us fame. And what is fame? Fame is the envy of the infamous. One is never famous for oneself. One is so only in relation to one's fellow-men. Let us take the trouble to observe the whirligig of everyday life from a bird's-eye view. There are women who adorn themselves like peacocks and cover themselves with finery and go swanking through the streets. Their diamonds, their furs, their silk dresses all proclaim: "I possess it, I possess it, I possess it. Do you see how much I possess? Are you not yellow with envy? I have still much more! To-morrow I shall come with other finery even more splendid." And the effect follows. Their sisters also want to be envied. Not for anything in the world would they speak the truth and betray that they are envious of the richer one. They want everything—but no pity. Envy only becomes silent before misfortune, and then it changes into pity. Oh, how some people gloat over pitying! The pity is not genuine; it is a secret rejoicing in another's sorrow. It shows one, with a secret feeling of pleasure, that there is now no need to envy one's neighbour. Yes, speech often discloses our secrets. In misfortune one sometimes says: "I do not envy the condition of the poor." How very clearly does the proverb, that inexhaustible source of fundamental wisdom, disclose it also: "Envy does not crawl in empty barns," or, "Better ten people envious than one pitiful"; "He who has no one envious of him, has no fortune."

Who has not noticed that people are always ready to sympathize in misfortune, and that they would rather weep with you a hundred times than rejoice with you once? There are people who never miss a burial service, and weep bitterly and are always full of sympathy. Besides the fact that these people are always bewailing their own lot, and so are glad when they get an excuse for weeping, they also have a feeling of relief that there is no need for envy. The sensation of being without envy is a gratifying, beautiful feeling, which can be compared with no other sensation. Those people who do not envy others are the best, because they have what most people lack; joy in their own possession.

How happy are those few who can feel joy in their own possession. They are proud of everything they possess. Their home, their little garden, their wife, their husband and their children, everything seems so valuable to them that they would not envy a king for all his riches. They are in reality the only rich people. To be rich means, in the noblest sense of the word, to be free of envy. Diogenes, who was satisfied with his tub and his sunshine, was the richest of men; anyway, much more so than was Croesus. He who has attained freedom from envy—and all of noble character should strive for this—is the first to notice the strength of others' envy. And the stronger he finds it, and the more he feels himself to be envied, the more is he astonished at the evil instincts which possess humanity.

There are also false proverbs. One hears over and over again that a happy and successful person has friends, and that misfortune drives friends away. "Every one will become your friend in good fortune." But this proverb is not in agreement with fact. Poverty drives away one's friends. "When you are in need, a hundred friends go to one ounce." But misfortune is not always poverty. Where there is no occasion for envy or need for help, there people force their friendship on you. But fortune and success drive friends away.

If one could only go by the assurances of people, one would be surrounded by the most faithful of friends. But, with a few rare exceptions, they are all secretly envious; enemies in disguise; and when the opportunity occurs they easily become open opponents. The more successful one is, and the greater one's fortune, the lonelier is one's life. One friend after another leaves the holy temple of friendship under the slightest pretexts. The friendship of him who is himself successful, you may be able to retain. He on whom no ray of success shines, must possess a rare magnanimity of soul, if he remains with his friend without envy.

What experiences the great have had! What horrible, horrible insight into the depths of human life! You can understand now the ostracism of the Athenians. A man was banished because he was too good and people liked him too much. This ostracism still to-day claims its victims. You feel yourself surrounded by secret enemies, although your intentions are noble and pure. You see one friend after another disappear from your society, and you question yourself in silent hours if perhaps you have not been a good friend to them yourself, or if you have given them some offence, or done them some harm? And the obscurity of unconscious feelings yields to a cold, cruel light. It is through no fault of yours that you have lost your friends, but it is because you have been successful and have fought your way through. They were too weak to confess to themselves openly that they could not bear your happiness. They looked out for pretexts and they found them. (Who could not find pretexts if he looked for them?) You have not greeted them in so friendly a way as usual. You have become proud. You have found other friends. The bitter truth is: they have never been sufficiently your friends to be able to enjoy your happiness with you without envy. You have given them insufficient cause for pity and compassion. They would far rather be your friends in need than be envious of your happiness. If we have sufficiently appreciated the importance of envy for the individual, we must not forget the tremendous social importance of envy. How fortunate it is that wishes cannot kill! How is it possible that people can be so foolish as to believe in the evil eye? A rich man who drives rapidly in his motor-car through the streets is followed by countless longing wishes of the less rich. The rays of envy pierce through the illuminated, cut-glass windows and play round the oblivious, joyous passengers. But these rays melt away ineffectually, and only increase the pride of the wealthy occupants.

One could write volumes about social envy. Let us illustrate it by a generally intelligible (so to say "popular") example. So much is said about the ingratitude of servants, and housewives never tire of illustrating this by the most incredible stories. Why do we expect gratitude and recognition? Over and over again I have observed that faithful servants can be found, with rare exceptions, only in poor families, where the servant can pity the wife and need not envy her. Happy people are unfortunate in their servants. Involuntarily, the servant class is consumed by envy. The maid envies her mistress her dresses, her pleasures and her freedom. Why? Is she not prettier than her mistress? Is she carved from a different wood? Is she not also a human being? Why should the other possess everything, and she herself be without? Women who have at one time been servants themselves can neither manage nor keep a servant. The servants will never reconcile themselves to having to serve her. Only high-born people can have real servants, and never those parvenus who have succeeded in obtaining what all servants long for: freedom from the fate of helots and promotion to the position of masters. That is the explanation of the secret solidarity of the servant class. They feel themselves united in hatred toward the mistresses whose bread they eat. For trifling reasons, hatred breaks out and they leave their mistresses, who have lavished upon them every kindness. And they take good care that the "lady" remains for a long time without servants. They tell all their complaints to the housekeeper and to the servants in the neighbourhood, and take good care to malign their mistress. They take a malicious pleasure in the knowledge that the "lady" has to do the work herself, and use her own hands. Just let her for once thoroughly enjoy the delights of work! This hatred is generally directed towards those women who do no work, and pass through life like drones. Working mistresses suffer much less from the envy of their servants.

A great many of the annoyances of life arise from this inexhaustible fount of envy. How should it not be so? Does not envy count as one of the seven deadly sins, which religion tried to do away with when it made love of one's neighbour the highest command? Should not the endeavours of all ethical thought be able to drive envy away, and to increase the joy in one's own possessions?

A great mistake is certainly made in our education. Every man is born an absolute egoist. But need he remain so? Rosegger says very truly: "The first, the very first sign of life which the awakening soul in a young human being utters is a revelation of self-love. Whether love for humanity will arise from it, or self-love—education will decide." Let us glance back at our early youth and remember the educational maxims of the first years in life, and of later periods. Always one heard: "Just look at Johnny, see what a good boy he is. What a joy he is to his parents!" We have always been educated by the example of others. Our vision has always been directed outward. It should go inward, and make use of the strength of one's own soul. It leads to an over-estimation of the other person. What we lack we seek in others. Our own incapacity for happiness causes our neighbour to appear happy to us. The knowledge of our own weakness makes us imagine strength in others. Everything we lack is possessed by the other. We seek it in the other instead of in ourselves. We are lacking in self-contentment and in the joy of our own ego. Because we rejoice too little in our own qualities, that which we possess becomes worthless. We lose self-esteem because we overvalue the other person and undervalue ourselves. New prospects are opened up into the psychology of the Ego which are well worth a closer investigation.

We must therefore endeavour to increase the joy in our own possessions and thus meet envy. Emerson was once asked why he did not travel about in order to see the beauties of the world. He answered: "Why should I seek the beauties of foreign places when I have not even exhausted the beauties of my own garden?" In this fertile ground grows the most noble quality of humanity; love to one's neighbours. Real love does not know envy. It is glad at the advantages possessed by others, and can rejoice in others' happiness. At any rate it can bear it.

Here shines a torch with which we can illuminate the dark nights of the present, and brighten the future. There is too little love in our world. We must educate our children in a love that uplifts one above oneself. Wherever the gentle, friendly rays of love penetrate, the yellow worm of envy disappears, creeping impotently away.

How many more thousand years will have to pass on towards eternity before the sun of love will shine over this world? At present the dark clouds of envy overshadow the splendid planet. Only now and then a bright ray breaks through the gloomy mist, and fills the trembling heart with secret hope.

CHAPTER XII

ARTISTS IN LIFE

THERE is one problem with which all thinking men particularly concern themselves: their attitude towards life. Over and over again we hear their catchword, "view of life"; and certainly the necessity to become quite clear about one's own line of direction is very general. We not only want to know what to make of the world and of life, we also want to be satisfied that we have tackled life rightly. There dwells in some dark corner of our soul a doubt which continually repeats the same questions to us: "Are you on the right way?" "Do you live your life as it should be lived?" and the third, and most important question of all: "Have you exhausted all possibilities of life?" repeatedly pass the threshold of consciousness. We all feel that life is a difficult art and we talk rightly of "Artists in Life." And by doing this we only show how far the great majority of men lack this art, because we select only a few to whom we give this title of "Artists in Life."

If we glance at those who are called "Artists in Life" by their fellows, we notice that they are mostly people who are able to gain from life the maximum amount of pleasure. They are those who demand for their capital of life energy the highest possible rate of interest. A somewhat deeper analysis very soon convinces us that these great capitalists of life-joy are living on interest at usurer's rate, and that there is nothing more dangerous than to over-exploit one's life force and to drain to the dregs the cup of enjoyment.

Every pleasure becomes a duty by repetition, and from the rose wreath of pleasure-feelings the sharp thorns of displeasure become apparent. A superfluity of enjoyment produces dullness; "Artists in Life" frequently become "blasé." The sad part of it is that these so-called "Artists in Life" are really no "Life Artists" at all. On the contrary, they are often miserable dabblers in life, and behind the mask of Life-Art there appears either the spectre of dissatisfaction, or that of boredom, or the tortured, suffering mien of neurosis and of "Weltschmerz." The so-called artists appear on closer investigation to be the poorest of mountebanks. They are mostly those people who feel themselves under the oppressing obligation to make the most of time, and kill it. Time is not only money for them, time is for them also enjoyment and pleasure. They are tortured by the horrible dread of the empty hours, when one becomes conscious of time. They wish neither to know, nor to feel, that they are growing older and are nearing death. They cannot hear the ticking of the great clock of life without shuddering. Every second which passes away into Eternity is to them a disturbing admonition and warning: "How have you spent life?" They gasp under the burden of living. They wrestle with life, and plunder time. They want to exhaust all possibilities of existence. They are always hunting for sensations; and they weave visions of future enjoyment, while the present pleasures only stir them slightly. They always want something *different*, they always think of something *different*, they always sacrifice to something *different*. They are always on the move, and are never satisfied. Although they are envied by those who are not in the secret, they feel that they are only tools of an extraneous motive force, and that for them pleasure is a labour, and work no pleasure.

It is not difficult to trace the individual variations of these types. The lady who must be present at every function, and neglects her house and family, who fights strenuously, and will take any amount of trouble in order to be present at a sensational law-suit, or at an important " first night." This lady who does " everything," is quite wrongly called an " Artist in Life." She really belongs to those miserable helots of society life who forget, amid their countless obligations, the most important duty, to think of one's self.

Another type is the young man, and the elderly man, who must try to play the part of the "smart fellow." I know highly moral people who feel a moral obligation to be immoral. The made up "smart man" is only a Philistine acting the Bohemian. He is under the obligation to be always merry. He is the man who must be present and show off his wit at every "rag." He has always to be cheerful at the behest of society. He can amuse and organize by request, and he invests himself with the halo of the man who is well acquainted with all human affairs. He has to play the part of the "Artist in Life." To his halo of the "smart fellow" he sacrifices his entire inner man, his needs and his secret inclination. How many people who are really ill " bleed to death " in secret in order to pass as healthy!

A third type of the false "Artist in Life" is the man who has time for everything. He is interested in a thousand things, and has a thousand things to do. At the portals of every hour there are waiting innumerable alternatives which thrust themselves forward: "Have you now time for me?" calls one. "No, for me," says another alluringly. In one sense the man is certainly happy; he does not know what boredom is. The day is short, and life passes only too quickly; behind him there is a demon (or is it his genius?) who drives him to work with the whip of the Sense of Duty. He is the man to whom people put the question, "How do you find the time to do it?" (All think it a miracle that he can do all that he does.) And the solution is very simple. This "Artist in Life" really does not live at all. He does not attain the conscious realization of his life. He staggers along in a constant state of intoxication with life, which, however, is not the same thing as really living. To really live one's life it is necessary to be conscious of living, and to know why, and for what purpose, one lives. These "Artists in Life" are not happy. Happiness depends upon knowing that one is able to use all one's capabilities in the right direction; happiness is also the ability to live in accordance with one's disposition, impulses and dreams.

Now what happens to those people who thus wear themselves out in their struggle against time? They never know happiness at all, because it only exists for them in the future; in the fulfilment of a plan which has hardly begun to be fulfilled when already new plans, new wishes and new duties appear. Such people are ingenious in saddling themselves with so many duties, a burden under which another person would break down. They belong to societies, they appear in public, they represent social functions in the world of politics, they busy themselves with art and nature, in short, they are everywhere and nowhere.

Another type of "Artist in Life" is that person who knows how to be lazy with dignity and enjoyment. To be lazy is not as easy as some simple-minded people imagine. One must have an innate talent for laziness. There are some remarkable people who know how to do nothing with great virtuosity, while giving the impression that they not only do something, but do even a great deal. They are extremely clever at keeping up an appearance of great deeds. They are like those pseudo-athletes who play Hercules and go through the actions of lifting tremendously heavy weights, while they handle only giant dumb-bells made of papier mâché. They pretend to sweat, and wipe their dry foreheads with a scented pocket-handkerchief.

Are they really "Artists in Life?" Do they not lack the most important thing, the backbone which keeps a man up, self-esteem? Do they not miss the delightful, priceless knowledge of their own value? Do they not fail to attain satisfaction with their own work? They are secretly admonished by an inner voice, which will not be silenced; that dear, but tiresome voice, seductive, and yet not to be deceived, which we call conscience!

We can see from these examples, to which many others could be added, that "Artists in Life" are very few and far between. Is there really such a thing as an "Artist in Life?" Was the poet Platen right in singing:

> Wer wusste je das Leben recht zu fassen,
> Wer hat die Hälfte nicht davon verloren,
> Im Traum, im Fieber, im Gespräch mit Toren,—
> In Liebesqual, im leeren Zeitverprassen?
>
> Denn jeder hofft doch, dass das Glück ihm lache,—
> Allein das Glück, wenn's wirklich kommt, ertragen—
> Ist keines Menschen, wäre Gottes Sache.

Who has ever grasped life in its fullness? Is there one who has not lost the half of it in dreams, in feverishness, in talking with fools, in lovesickness, in reckless squandering of time? Although every one hopes that Fortune may smile on him; yet, should Fortune really come—no human, only divine Beings could bear it.

And how sad is the continuation of the sonnet where Platen denies every possibility of happiness.

Is there then no such thing as the "Art of Life," and are there no "Artists in Life?" Must we look for examples of happiness to the animals of the woods, and the simple in mind? Does then the fact of not pondering over life constitute the "Art of Life;" and are those people whom we call "Dabblers in Life" the artists?

No, no, we cannot go altogether by the poets. We know them. We know what unsatisfied fellows they are, and that it is just their misfortunes and their dissatisfaction with the world that forces them to create and work. They work for other people, who enjoy the productions which have been brought forth with pain and anguish, with doubt and anxiety. *Aus meinen grossen Schmerzen mach' ich die kleinen Lieder.* ("Out of my deep sorrows, I make my little songs.") But there must be a real "Art of of not pondering over life constitute the "Art of Life"; The secret consists in the harmonious interchange of work and enjoyment. They are people for whom work is a pleasure; but who, nevertheless, are capable of calling an emphatic halt from time to time. They are people who possess the ability to relax and to disconnect. People often possess the former, but of what use is relaxation if the mind does not possess the capability of disconnecting? Without forgetting there is no enjoyment of the present.

How full of meaning and true to life is the idea of the ancients, that we must drink of the waters of Lethe before we can reach the Fields of the Blessed! Man must always carry with him this magic Water of Forgetfulness in order to be able to enjoy life. There is also a "forgetting" which is pathological, because it fixes those emotions of which we have never become fully conscious, and retains them in the depths of our souls. We can only forget that of which we have actually been conscious. Grillparzer advises every one who wishes to become thoroughly sound, to go on thinking out every unpleasant thought till he finds a solution in the intellect. And Feuchtersleben, the great doctor and thinker, holds that one must master an object before one may despise it. That which is brushed aside, continually reappears with ever-increasing obstinacy. Only the light of day can, by elucidating them, disperse all the spectres of night. To put these theories into practice, we should be forced to bring all painful thoughts to a solution. But there are so many unpleasant thoughts which can never be dealt with conclusively. Every one has open wounds that will not heal, and through which one secretly "bleeds to death." But does not this probing of the wounds cause greater pain than if one allowed them to heal of themselves? There are wounds of the soul which the surgeon's cold and cruel knife must explore. Others are healed by peace and by time.

Only the "Artist in Life" can forget all when the hour demands it. He possesses the ability to disconnect. If he is at a concert, he forgets his business and his worries; in business he only lives for his work. He does everything whole-heartedly, because owing to his power of disconnecting he can concentrate on the present time and on the moment. He drives away care and so is able to enjoy the present because the past does not oppress him. That is the deepest secret of the art of life: to sever the strings which tie us to the world of displeasure, and to enjoy every minute as if it offered to us what it had never offered before. By such concentrated and concentric thinking, the ordinary man can develop all his capabilities. The "Artist in Life" can do even more. He can even forget that he has capabilities. He can enjoy himself and listen to the voices in his innermost soul, without the intrusion of alien thoughts and sad memories.

Thus should the true "Artist in Life" be. Go and seek him! Seek him in the noise of the great town, or in the quiet of the country! I am afraid you would fare like the dying king, to whom the doctors promised recovery if he could put on the shirt of a happy man. His servants and counsellors searched for a long time in vain throughout the kingdom to find one happy person. At last they found one, but this happy man had no shirt! Also this "Artist in Life" might be found rather in a hut than in a palace. The "Art of Having no Needs" is a part of the "Art of Life." To be interested in everything, to possess a wide circle of interests and of work, to be able to forget when the hour of rest demands it, to be able easily to renounce what one has eagerly desired, and not to consume oneself in longing for the unattainable, that is the real "Art of Life." Who would be able to fulfil all this? We must be content to strive for the ideal. The very fact of striving for art implies in itself a great deal of art.

CHAPTER XIII

THE UNLUCKY DOG

It is always just to him that it happens! It is as if Fate had chosen, among all human beings, one special Unfortunate in order to heap upon his poor head all the misfortunes of existence. If one listens to the jeremiads of such an "Unlucky Dog," his life consists of an unbroken chain of unpleasant, deliberately cruel events which are heaped upon him. All his friends are lucky enough, but he is followed by quite special, unbelievable, unprecedented ill-luck. Whatever he touches goes wrong. Every hope ends in disappointment. Every joy is spoilt for him. In short, he is an "Unlucky Dog."

Are there really these unfortunates who have such exquisite ill luck? What does it mean to have ill luck?

One must not judge according to one's first impressions, because if one listens to this astonishing series of special misfortunes, of plans which failed, of wasted endeavours, one is almost convinced that life does treat different people differently: it empties its cornucopia liberally over some, whilst, like the spiteful stepmother, it puts stumbling-blocks in the way of others. But on closer investigation one may find a hidden force which is guiding his Fate. To use a popular phrase, there are people who run to have their ears boxed.

We might learn from the wise words of Goethe that the secret of good fortune lies in the power to grasp it. "*Wozu in die Ferne schweifen?—Sieh, das Gute liegt so nah:—Lerne nur das Glück ergreifen—und das Glück ist immer da.*" (Why roam in the far distance? See, how near the Good lies! Only learn how to grasp happiness, and happiness is always there.)

Does not this mean that equal chances are offered to all human beings? That we each have the power to find the Good; that we are unhappily blind to what is near, and seek for the Good in the far distance, where it can never be found? Such an "Unlucky Dog" must possess a special faculty for concealing his capabilities. The reason why he is such an unlucky dog lies in the foundations of his psychic constitution. And our task now is to trace back the connexions. Each of us is anxious not to be swallowed up in the crowd of ordinary humanity, like everybody else. Each would stand above the others, would be conspicuous, and would attain to something quite exceptional. And every one has deep in his soul the secret hope that he will succeed in working himself up and enforcing his Ego upon others. But in course of time, when one realizes that the claims of the "great historical mission" cannot be fulfilled, then one seeks for an excuse, outside oneself, for the breaking down of all one's hopes.

What could be easier than to blame blind Fate for it? It was not our fault that we did not get on better; we have had ill-luck. Our friends who have been successful simply had "good luck." Thus the depressing feeling of inferiority is entirely removed. It is no longer necessary to admit to oneself: You did not get on better because you were lazy, or because you were lacking in capability. No, you have simply had ill-luck. You never do have any luck. . . .

These "tendencies to excuse oneself" play a great part in human life, and especially in the life of the neurotic. He has a tendency to project outwardly all the events of his psyche, to see them, so to say, objectively, and only then to bring them into relationship with his own Ego. For example, Mr. A. is in a bad humour, for which he blames the bad weather. How could he be cheerful on such a grey day? He forgets that yesterday, in spite of blue skies, he was also in bad spirits, for which he laid the blame on a letter he had received from a friend. The day after to-morrow perhaps some news in the newspaper will depress him. He will be very unwilling to admit that it is his own bad mood, his own unhappiness which he projects into the world, and which returns to him now in the form of unpleasurable impressions.

The "Unlucky Dog" projects his shortcomings on to Fate, making ill-luck the excuse for his own weakness. At the same time, this tendency to distinguish himself from the crowd breaks through. He is not an ordinary unlucky dog; he is quite an exceptional one. Good Lord! Many people have misfortunes, but nobody else has such special misfortunes as he. That had already begun when he was at school. If for once it should have happened that he had not learned one little part of his lesson, the teacher would be certain to pitch on just this particular part on which to question him. If he goes for an excursion, it is sure to rain. If he goes to an inn, he upsets his stomach. If he goes by train, the train is either late, has a collision, or some other accident. And his illness!—Who has ever heard of a person getting appendicitis from a cup of tea? Yet he was the unfortunate person who did so. And what a serious operation it was that he had! Everything had grown together, and his life hung by a thread. To cap everything, two days after the operation, his surgeon became ill, and was obliged to send another one in his place, who messed about with him, and did not understand the case at all! And so it goes on, and he is not satisfied until he has convinced his listeners and made them thoroughly realize that he is really an exceptionally unlucky dog. When he has succeeded in this, one can see a smile of satisfaction pass over his face. He has obtained his wish, and has succeeded in being quite an "exceptional person."

But what is the real truth of this story? Are they all lies which he told? Or is there a certain amount of truth in his complaints? I have now to take our poor unfortunate's part. He did not lie, but has only over-emphasized and exaggerated, as all story-tellers involuntarily do. The art of story-telling lies chiefly in the touching-up. But who ever has been always lucky in life? Who has always been successful? Who has never had to complain about the spitefulness of the object? Life presents itself in different ways according to how one emphasizes the lucky or unlucky events. The "unlucky dog" goes through the same experiences as the person born under a lucky star. But he relates only stories which are in a minor key. He has merely forgotten all the lucky events of his life. This illustrates the instructive story of the knife and fork.

It is a story which had always puzzled me as a boy. We had a drawer, in the dark depths of which knives and forks were hidden from sight. When I was told to take out a fork, of course my hand brought out a knife. When I was told to get a knife, invariably a fork, with a handle similar to that of a knife, came to my hand. This spitefulness of the object caused me to make a record of the successes and the failures in my searches. Greatly to my surprise, the successes and the failures balanced each other. I then realized that I had not observed those occasions when I had been successful, but had overlooked them because there was nothing to bring them into notice.

There are many people who appear to be continually harassed by misfortune. These have a peculiar knack of never forgetting the bad things. They manage to forget the good things quickly enough, but the memory of all the unpleasant things remains indelibly. They are people who do not easily forgive either themselves or others, and least of all Fate, if things are not to their liking. Only a noble nature can forget the ill done, even by one's enemy. The "Unlucky Dog," one will discover from his conversation, has not forgotten any evil thing which has ever occurred to him. He has not forgotten the curt answer given him ten years ago, nor an insignificant dispute in his youth, nor a pointed remark of a friend, nor an unjust reproach from his teacher. He keeps an exact account of all his unpleasant memories; he keeps a careful daily record of them, and is most anxious that not one of them should be lost. All the good things in life that have come to him just as much as to any one else—his success, his joys, his strokes of luck—he forgets as soon as possible, or else he tries to remember some unpleasant occurrence coincident with his good fortune. If for once it really occurred that he was fortunate, then something exceptional was sure to have happened at the same time to spoil the enjoyment of his luck.

In this way is often formed a strange superstition, which although sometimes very cleverly disguised is at others quite evident. He behaves as if he lived in fear of ill-luck, which might be brought upon him by one or other of his actions. He dare not enjoy himself because experience has shown him that then something evil always happens. As pleasant and unpleasant impressions must alternate with each other, so a stroke of luck is sure to be followed by something less enjoyable. The " Unlucky Dog," believing in secret supernatural powers which govern his fate, is afraid of these spectres and does not want to provoke them. There is already apparent, even in this superstition which he hardly admits to himself, a tremendous feeling of self-importance. He is followed by ill-luck; that signifiies, according to his own superstition, that there are supernatural powers who take a particular delight in selecting him for their persecution and mockery. Occasionally a glimmer of truth breaks into his mind: he imagines his ill-luck to be a punishment—a punishment for his evil thoughts. He does not deserve good fortune. A deep feeling of guilt hinders him from being happy. He feels that he is not a good man, and deserves no better fate.

Sometimes he has a revelation of his own badness. When does this occur? Whenever he hears of other people's misfortunes. Then his secret delight in the misfortunes of other people, his brutal egoism and his hidden cruelty become apparent to him. While on a visit he hears that his cousin's child has had to be taken to the South on account of hip disease, and that the disease will probably be one of many years' duration. His first impulsive thought is, " Why shouldn't he have something to worry him for once?" This cousin of his, having been more successful in business, was very much envied by him. His first impulse, therefore, on hearing the unhappy news, is one of malicious joy. But after a few minutes he feels that this malicious joy is a sin, a low impulse. He says to himself, "You really are a bad lot! You certainly do not deserve that things should go well with you." And now the door is open for ill-luck, the well-deserved punishment for the evil stirrings of his mind. Now the voice of conscience forces him to look for misfortune. He purposely avoids all opportunity of meeting happiness and of enjoying himself. He is an "unlucky dog," as he wishes to be.

A great part is played by a barely admitted piety. We all know the strange teaching that it is more difficult for a rich man to enter heaven than for a camel to pass through the eye of a needle. Which means in other words: if you have enjoyed yourself on earth, you will suffer for it in another world. The "unlucky dog" hopes for happiness in the other world. His life has been a chain of misfortune. Should he not then gain compensation for his sufferings, and acquire eternal blessedness? The idea of redemption through suffering is deeply engraved in the race consciousness. Among the "unlucky dogs" there are more martyrs than freethinkers, who bear their misfortune with resignation and humour. There is another point: unhappy people are always sure of compassion. We have now arrived at an important point in the psychology of this subtle gentleman. He is thirsting for love. He feels himself at a disadvantage in the great love market of life, and seeks love in the form in which it is most easily obtainable. As he cannot obtain the gold of love, and the silver of friendship is denied him, he puts up with the copper of compassion, and that he tries to gain in such quantity as will compensate for gold and silver combined. He grabs it from every quarter, and by all means. No one is too insignificant for him to arouse to compassion by the story of his misfortune. He is a beggar for love, and rarely begs in vain, because people are only afraid lest they should be in the position of envying others. They are lavish enough with their compassion. The sorrows of others form a sombre background, throwing into relief the brightness of their own fortune.

That impulse which Krafft-Ebing calls Masochism, pleasure in one's own suffering, belongs to the darkest chapters in psychology. It is one of man's most remarkable achievements that he is capable of gaining pleasure from pain. It seems certain to me that this perverse form of reaction can only come about through the instrumentality of the feeling of guilt. For this reason, the animal world gives us no analogy for Masochism. The animal, in a state of freedom, knows no feeling of guilt; but in dogs and domesticated animals we observe a very marked feeling of guilt, even though he finds that he is not which they have been educated. A dog who, owing to illness, dirties the room, will show a distinct feeling of guilt even though he finds that he is not punished for his fault. Guilty feeling is due to the overruling of inhibitions with subsequent repentance. It has been left to man to transform guilt into pleasure! All masochists are repentant sinners, who punish themselves for indulgence in forbidden pleasures. But just as everything that King Midas touched became gold, so even punishment is turned into pleasure. This strange phenomenon of the displacement and distortion of pleasure can be even better shown in other examples than in that of the "Unlucky Dog."

We have pointed out that the "Unlucky Dog's" feeling of guilt originates from his evil wishes. These wishes produce a variation which is in reality the fundamental type, the "Unlucky Dog" who brings misfortune to others. There certainly are people who imagine that they bring ill-luck to their friends and acquaintances. Card players know of such unfortunate people who find difficulty in watching a game of cards, because of the ill-luck which they appear to bring. The people who believe they possess this unfortunate power are afraid to make friendships; they warn their acquaintances, and seem to be in a great state about it. I say they "seem," because behind their despair is hidden a good deal of secret megalomania. There are many neurotics who believe in the omnipotence of their thoughts, as is the belief of all children. Who would not like to be a magician, or has not feverishly devoured those fairy tales where fairies and magicians can fulfil every wish? A remnant of the old belief in magic still exists in man. We have often heard stories about the "evil eye," and there are still millions of people who believe this nonsense. Children are still being bewitched, the village woman puts a spell over the cattle to make them sick, and peaceful happiness is still destroyed by the "evil eye" of envious neighbours.

The "Unlucky Dog" possesses then the ability to bring misfortune to others, and that is his silent revenge for all the misfortune he has had to bear himself. He suffers, but he causes others also to suffer—or so he imagines to himself. He always manages to connect his own personality with the misfortunes of other people.

But shall we be angry with the poor "Unlucky Dog?" Let him slink unhappily through life, and whine about his misery!

We have seen through him. We do not believe in his misfortune, and we are not afraid of his presence. We want to go through life merrily; we want to be "dancers" in the sense suggested by the great world-wise Nietzsche. We do not want to have ill-luck, and so we do not have it. We know that everything is only vanity. Pleasure and displeasure, luck and ill-luck, success and defeat, triumph and humiliation, recognition and scorn, they all dance an eternal roundelay, and the best thing we can do is to join in the dance too. He who cannot do so is unfortunate; but let him just lift up his clumsy legs and try to dance. That's right, Unlucky Dog! Just go on! A little more practice, and you will change into a fat, little, lucky pig! Such a metamorphosis is not unheard of. Many a happiness has changed to misfortune, and many a misfortune has become happiness.

Nothing in itself is unfortunate; it all depends on the attitude we take. Every one can have luck if he looks for it. Luck means, as I have already mentioned before, to make other people's interests one's own! Luck means to adapt oneself to reality, and to make the most of all the possibilities the day brings. Luck means to live in others for oneself, and to live for others in oneself.

CHAPTER XIV

IMPATIENCE

TIME stretches before us immeasurable, incomprehensible and limitless, like a bridge stretching from eternity to eternity. But thought transcends space and time. Mankind cannot endure anything so great that it is beyond his comprehension. Therefore Time, the indivisible, is divided up and brought into the realm of consciousness in seconds, minutes, hours, days and years. Even a great river, with which Time is so often compared, has posts along its banks, on which the distances are marked. But the measurement applies only to the banks, and not to the stream, whose waters run on whilst we are watching them.

There is a curious relationship between time and mankind. And again every person has his individual relationship therewith, which considerably affects that phenomenon which we generally call character. Above everything else, the human mind protests against the scanty allowance of time, and against the finality of existence. He cannot, and will not, accept the fact that one day he will exist no longer, and time will be for other people to enjoy.

Religion always draws attention to the shortness of the time at our disposal, and gives a promise of eternal life, which, according to our behaviour on earth, will be either pleasurable or displeasurable. It is one of the most wonderful consolations of belief that it helps us over the problem of time.

Earthly happiness, or that condition which we call happiness, is primarily dependent upon our relationship to time. People who have no time, but, in spite of that, find time for everything they wish to do, are the happiest. There is no need for them to kill time. They never get so far as to become conscious of it—they know no boredom. Boredom is nothing else than consciousness of time. There are people who have not the courage to look time in the face. They must keep themselves occupied lest they should become aware of time; and for the same reason, they do not want to be alone. There is another spectre which hides behind this fear of boredom: fear of death. Every irrevocable second brings us nearer the grave.

To most people, the thought of dying and of the

end of existence, the sinking back into the lap of eternity, is unbearable. They are afraid of departing from this world before they have tasted to the last drop all the joys and wonders which it offers. How often the doctor hears the remark: "I do not want to die yet, I have had so little out of life!"

The impatient person's world differs from the world of the patient one, in so far as he who is impatient cannot wait for the fruit of his activities. He mistrusts time, and suspects it as a creditor does a bad debtor through whom he is afraid he will lose his money. He expects punctual payment, his interest, and the enjoyment of the fruits of his labour, and insists on his due. He is a Shylock who conducts usurious business with life. Time certainly is an excellent payer. It pays, but according to its whims, and does not like to be importuned. When least expected, it pays with interest and double interest; but to him who demands impatiently, with continual reminders of its obligations, it pays least. Ripe fruits fall into the hands of him who can wait, but many a failure in the life of the impatient man arises from the eagerness with which he hunts for success.

He who is impatient lives in a continual struggle with time. He does not want to become old, and does not want to be reminded of the grave. He does not want to have fulfilment only after the flames of longing have been extinguished. He wants to burn in the glow of life, and to exhaust every possible experience before it fades. Time is his perpetual adversary, who keeps him continually on the go, and never gives him any peace. The impatient man is everlastingly dissatisfied, and bewails his fate. But where shall we find a contented person nowadays?

There are two kinds of human beings: the patient and the impatient. And between these two great groups there are innumerable grades. There are the seemingly patient ones, whose hearts are burning with the desire for fulfilment, whilst they appear to be calm and quietly waiting; then there are the patient ones whose patience suddenly collapses, and they then become more wild than those who are impatient; they have become strong in the fight with time.

When one does not too eagerly demand, Time will pour out all the profusion of gifts he has to offer. Only in the poverty of wishing rests the wealth of fulfilment. Life sometimes goes like a fairy tale: a fairy appears, and crowns the contented one, proclaiming him a prince or king. But sometimes, in the decisive moment, it gently closes his eyes, and leads him into the mysterious land which lies beyond patience and impatience.

It is a peculiar trait in people, that they all carry a secret about with them, and yet are incapable of keeping this secret to themselves. They betray it in all their actions, in every movement of their body, in every word they speak, in their mien and gestures. It is absurd to disbelieve in graphology nowadays. One can tell a person's character not only by his handwriting, but also by his manner of walking, and by the way he looks at one. To take a very prosaic example: one can recognize our two types most easily in their manner of eating. The patient one will keep the best mouthful till the last; he increases the enjoyment by prolonging the "fore-pleasure" as much as possible. The impatient one seizes on the best bit as if in fear of its being taken from him. His enjoyment is in the retrospect; he is the man for "after-pleasure." We find the same type among the animals. The dog is impatient, and chooses from his meal the best piece first, and puts up with the less attractive portion afterwards. The cat is for "fore-pleasure." She plays long with the mouse before devouring it slowly and at ease.

The danger for the patient person lies in the over-estimation of "fore-pleasure." We discover that by his patience he gains a secret pleasure. Therefore the fulfilment is a disappointment for him, and he has good cause to put it off as long as possible. He has already enjoyed all the pleasure, and all his aim is only for the endeavour. The impatient one should really possess to the full the delights of the moment. But already, while enjoying, he is longing for new enjoyments. Memory remains to him as a treasured possession. He is the man who appears to be hurrying forward, and yet continually glances backward. He can never find what he seeks, because his future is his past, and the present must become the past before he can obtain enjoyment from it. Thus the conception of happiness finds its solution in two directions. The moment of happiness is without value for most people. Some seek only the memory of happiness, others the foretaste, but fewest of all can say to the present: "Verweile doch, du bist so schön!" ("Stay awhile; thou art so beautiful!") Faust is the type of the impatient one, who, full of a thousand schemes, pursues one enjoyment after another, and finally returns to youth. There is only one real happiness—childhood, when one was with the mother. But oh, the irony of Fate! At that time one did not realize one's happiness. It is the ideal of all human beings to be grown up and yet a child.

The impatient one's world is the world of childhood. Children are consumed with the desire to be old. The years stretch endless before them. If there is anything which could prove to us that time is never an absolute, but always a relative, concept, then it is certainly this misapprehension of time. To a lover waiting for his beloved, the seconds seem endless, and to the person condemned to death, the last hours pass like fleeting seconds. To the child, time seems like eternity. It passes all too slowly for him, and from one birthday to another is an immense period. For the old man, the years pass like the sounds of a distant song. Time is like a *trottoir roulant.* We believe we are moving ourselves and are only being moved. Or we are at a cinema, where one can travel round the world for a few pence. One passes rapidly through wonderful countries, and yet still remains on the same spot. The picture moves before our eyes, producing the optical illusion that it is we ourselves who are moving. So time passes us by, while we fondly imagine that we are passing time.

The impatient one wants to get the better of time by running a race with it. Finally he drops down exhausted, and that's the end of that little comedy. When pleasure called alluringly to him, he never had time for it. He rushed madly after success, and, in this wild chase, forgot life itself; forgetting that the real meaning of life is to live. He never had time to notice that time held him in its clutches, and played with him as a cat plays with a mouse.

If he loses patience and despairs of his success, then they say of him that he is nervy and has overworked himself. What silly talk! We never get nervy over work which we enjoy. Goethe holds that activity shortens time, and idleness makes it unbearably long. The impatient one does not love work for itself; he would rather obtain his aim without work. That is why he so often lives in a world of fantasies and is blind to realities. What he demands of time is unobtainable He would like to convert the value of his dreams into terms of reality. Fantasies mostly have a very low exchange value, insufficient for the purchase of reality. There is only one exception to this, the case of the artist. He alone can obtain money for his fantasies, and from the world of dreams he creates his greatest successes. He can transform all his impatience into works, and so fulfil his childhood wishes. In the sphere of art are still to be found those poor peasant boys who become kings, and before whom the great crowd bows.

What the impatient ones seeks is ruling power, that kingdom which is promised to us of old in fairy tales and by our own dreams. Why should he battle with the miseries of life, and be a poor clerk, or spend his life in selling goods behind a counter, while he is dreaming of crowns and precious stones? No, he does not renounce the value of his fantasies. He insists on his kingdom. And when his wishes have become bankrupt, and the share value of his fantasies have dwindled to nothing, a neurosis develops. Then he seeks refuge in another world, and this other world is neurosis, or, under certain conditions, madness.

Neurotics are impatient people who have lost patience. No one needs so much patience as the impatient one. The patient one needs no patience because it is already in him and he cannot lose it. The impatient one wastes like a spendthrift all the patience he has, and soon becomes a beggar. Then it is that he has to pick up the crumbs of what he has once carelessly thrown away. As Raimund tells us in his wise fairy tale, a beggar is following behind each of us. When we stretch out our hand in the greatest need, it is unexpectedly filled with treasures of the past, which life has compassionately held in store for us.

Then we try to rebuild a new home from the scanty remnants. And the great miracle is wrought; the impatient one learns to economize his patience, and eventually concludes an armistice with time, or perhaps even a lasting peace. He has learnt to put up with reality, and is content with what each day brings: the scent of a spring evening, the perfume of fresh mown hay, or a song dying away in the silence of the night. It is happiness enough!

CHAPTER XV

DEGENERATE CHILDREN

The increasing number of reports of child criminals have drawn universal attention to the relationship between degeneracy and childhood. Just recently we have read of a twelve-year-old thief, who in courage and cunning could not have been outdone by his oldest fellow-criminals. How do such moral abnormalities come into existence? Are they congenital? Are they acquired?

There is nothing more painful for parents than to see that a child that has been surrounded with love, and brought up with every care, has fallen into wrong ways, and has begun to be accounted a failure. They anxiously ask themselves where the blame lies. They spared no trouble with regard to his education, shunned no expense and obtained the help of expensive tutors and foreign governesses. The one aim of their lives, which for years had been ever before them, was that their child might have a splendid future; no ideal was too high. But what disappointment time brought! Gradually they saw all their proud hopes dwindle, until they would have been thankful to have seen even a little talent, instead of the anticipated genius. But to whatever modest proportions they might reduce their desires, the reality was invariably disappointing.

One can hardly believe what an utter devil a beloved and charming child, who has been the joy of his family, may become. Gradually the wings fall off, and step by step the idolized child becomes the tormenting tyrant of the house, enforcing all his changing wishes, which become ever more monstrous the more easily he finds they are carried out. At first the child is counted as spoilt, then as naughty, and at last it has to be admitted that he is different from normal children; he is what pedagogues call a failure, and doctors call degenerate. An excellent expression has been coined by Koch for such children as stand on the boundary between health and disease—" Psycho-Pathological Inferiorities."

The type of which such a degenerate child is an example, is not a rigid one, there are numberless variations—nevertheless it will not be difficult to sketch its character in a few strong lines. He is, before all things, boundlessly egoistic (" Hypertrophy of the

Ego "), all altruistic feelings are to him inconceivable and incomprehensible. If he professes these feelings, then behind this is hidden one of the small dissimulations in which he is such an adept. His comfort, his desires count above everything with him. First comes the beloved Ego, and then all others. He is jealous, because in every token of love shown to another child his egoism detects a betrayal of the affection due to him, and to him alone. He is easily offended, and of uncontrolled temper, and so incessantly comes into conflict with his brothers, sisters and school-fellows. For this reason he seldom has a friend, but, on the contrary, many enemies with whom he comes to blows, or has other violent scenes. He always feels himself persecuted as the scapegoat. Either the teacher is " down on him," or the school children have conspired against him, or one or other of his relations is waiting for an opportunity to persecute him. He is changeable and restless and cannot stick at anything for any length of time. Such children change the school that they attend almost every year, because the parents are only too willing to believe the child's complaints, and the unjust persecution of the poor child appears to them as a plausible and sufficient excuse for bad school reports. Degenerate children are insubordinate to teachers and parents, and, in fact, recognize no authority; at the same time they lack all self-confidence. They are always dependent upon extra coaching and special tutors, and make themselves conspicuous by an endless series of misdemeanours. As a rule they are dirty and very greedy, devour their food hastily and can never have enough. They can often be convicted of lying, intriguing and even of small thefts. They like to threaten suicide, which they go so far as to simulate occasionally in a very clever way. If one is not complaisant to their wishes they also threaten other deeds of violence—for instance, arson. What a long catalogue of failings! Fortunately, every degenerate child does not fully exhibit the whole of these bad qualities. As already mentioned, there are numerous variations. Often the above-mentioned qualities are only slightly marked, or only break out at certain intervals. There is one symptom, however, which we have not mentioned, which is common to all degenerate children; it is a conspicuous sexual precocity, a strong accentuation of erotic emotions.

It is touching to see how some parents fret themselves in their endeavours to bring such degenerate children into right ways, and how, in the simplicity of their hearts, they often employ the most erroneous methods, whereby they further strengthen the evil qualities of the child and lose the good ones altogether. This can readily be understood when one investigates the foundations of such abnormalities. There is much talk in these days of degeneration and heredity. That there has been enormous exaggeration in this respect has been proved by the recent investigations of outstanding psychiatrists and psychologists. But one factor cannot be over emphasized—that is then environment. One can hardly expect morally sound descendants from criminal families, from drunkards of the real, downright dipsomaniac type (not temperate drinkers). And, naturally, orphans, or children whose parents are busy the whole day away from home, become degenerate more easily than those children who are watched over by the loving eye of the mother. But he who would imagine that this alone is sufficient to avert degeneracy, or the formation of moral insanity, would be very much mistaken. For we very often find degenerate children just in the best of families where children are watched over and brought up with exaggerated care. Here also, if one investigates further, the environment will be found to be the fundamental cause. What sort of marriages are those in which we find such child failures? They are usually so-called unhappy marriages, which lack that harmonious atmosphere of a peaceful home which is necessary for the development of a healthy soul. The father and mother are continually quarrelling with each other for a thousand reasons—because they did not marry for love, or because they love each other too much; because one or the other is neurotic, and the neurosis explodes into countless domestic storms, because the man or the woman is unfaithful, and so forth. But why repeat what is common knowledge? At an early age the child is drawn into these conflicts. "You belong to me alone, and you are only to love me!" cries the irate mother in a pathetic tone, clasping the child convulsively to her breast. "You have got to do only what I tell you!" shouts the father. "I am master of this house!" And secretly he asks the child if he does not love him better than Mummy.

The foundation-stone of degeneracy is laid. The child knows no authority in the home. The first authority that the child gets to know is the father. Round about this belief in authority are built all those moral restraints that are necessary to the individual in order that he may fulfil his social duties and not come into conflict with written and unwritten laws. It is told of Carrière, the famous French painter, who died not long ago, that he had made the remark that the education of youth must begin with the undermining of all authority. Theoretically, that may be very beautifully thought out; actually, it is impossible and impracticable. We haven't got as far as that yet; we have not yet reached that ethical height. In other words, children have not yet reached that stage where ethics can replace authority. Undoubtedly many individual children have got as far as that; but the great mass of mankind will not have reached this stage even in a thousand years. For the present, education must begin with authority, and freedom must be won by the individual himself overcoming the belief in authority.

Certainly no authority can be gained by means of violence and blows; there is only one way—a living example. In a family in which peace and harmony rule, in a family where the will both of the father and of the mother are mutually respected, in such a family there will hardly ever be a degenerate child; for education begins with a belief in the authority of the parents, and with an intense wish to become like father and mother. On this broad foundation must be built all that goes to the making of the moral man. In rare cases, the tutor or the governess may be able to play this part, because the most powerful lever of education is, and always will be, love. Not that ape-like love—blind, exaggerated, unmeasured, neurotic, which the cultured modern person shows; but the quiet, deep love that sees faults more clearly than the stranger even, and does not turn virtues into affected conceit by boundless praise. Apish love gives the child whatever it wants, and believes in this way to make it happy. This is truly a bad preparatory school for life. The child very easily gets into the way of thinking that every wish is realizable if he has found that he has obtained most of his desires by cunning and tears. It is more important to train a child to renounce than to enjoy.

Educationalists are able to say more about this subject than doctors, who only come in contact with the results of this false education. Connected with this subject are also the so-called pleasures of children. A child must have free play for its imagination. A piece of wood stimulates its imagination more than the most beautiful doll with splendid clothes. The faithful likeness to Nature of the modern manufactured toy is the reverse of a benefit to humanity; just as objectionable for children are the various children's plays in theatres, with their fairy stories staged with extravagant splendour—ballets, concerts, *e tutti quanti.* What is there left for the child to long for? And the longing for the unknown and the new is the most powerful lever to progress, as much for the individual as for the whole of humanity.

It need not here be expected that I shall start on the usual Jeremiad against schools and institutions, against Latin and Greek, etc., but I must mention one thing: it is not every one who is cut out for study. Thousands of unfortunate youths who would have made excellent artisans, capable business men and efficient farmers, arrive at nothing in secondary schools, and become unstable drifters, because they have been sacrificed by the stupidity of their parents to an ambitious project for a "cultured" profession. The art of the educator is chiefly shown in his treatment of slightly abnormal children. One seldom finds a child that has not a great interest—and even a certain talent—for some occupation, or another. Here the natural disposition must be exploited to the fullest extent. Years ago, I drew attention to the law of re-valuation of mental energies. The most frequent cause of delinquency is a surplus of energy which cannot discharge itself, and therefore breaks out as mischief or bad conduct. One often sees a wonderful change when such children get work which is agreeable to them, and the modern method of dealing with them is based on this. The so-called reformatories, that were formerly so much favoured, are in fact really dangerous, just because the children meet with so many evil and depraved companions that they become yet more infected with moral poison, and in the end their psychological training results only in the power to deceive more cleverly.

Quite different are the modern educational establishments which try to attain their aim by work and by the awakening of their sense of appreciation for Nature. In this way, the surplus energy is provided with a suitable channel, and the body is hardened by outdoor life. At the same time, the sense of the beauty of the universe is aroused, and the effort is made to influence the psyche through the example of the teacher, who is to the pupil in the relationship not of a tyrant, but of a friend. Unfortunately, there are but very few institutions like that founded in Zurich by the engineer Grohmann.

Finally, the child finds in life itself his best teacher. I have before me many examples where so-called delinquent children grew to be exemplary and blameless persons, and useful members of society. Independence is often the best means of lending a certain stability to such unstable beings. But even there one may generalize. Hundreds overcome their youthful disability, and, recovering psychic health, climb upwards on the social ladder; again, hundreds disappear in the turbid stream which we call life.

No mechanical method can be employed for the handling of degenerate children. Pedagogic prescriptions of universal validity do not exist. Here, every case must be treated and solved individually.

The field of prophylaxis is much more fruitful. In this connexion a very striking story of Multatuli occurs to me that has been published in his *Ideen* under the title of "Prophylaxis." It relates how a young girl of modest, pious and housewifely upbringing was brought by her family for entrance into a lunatic asylum. The lady in charge of the female patients in the institution said to the family: "Our rules for treatment are simple. Gentleness is the chief thing. After that, naturally, of course, come light, air, plenty of change, exercise, suitable amusements. . . ." On the way home, the family of the poor patient discussed these rules of treatment, and a younger sister said to the father, "Light, air, change, exercise, suitable amusements! . . . But, Father, if only we had begun with these before our poor sister became mad?"

Multatuli goes on to say that he does not know what this father answered, but in his opinion, it had been better for him to have had a millstone tied about his neck (and more still) one second before his marriage, than to have had to hear such a question from the lips of his child, than to *deserve* such a question from his child. There are *many* such fathers for whom he would recommend a millstone.

Multatuli is cruel. The father acted only through lack of understanding, and not with evil intention. It is the evil intention only that should be punished.

But a deep truth lies in the little satire of this great poet and philanthropist. It should not be difficult for parents to deduce the wise teaching from it. The life of the child must be writ in joy, and full of variety. His teaching should come through his play, and instruction should be play to him. At home, he should only know the sunny side of life. Certainly, social circumstances often make this impossible, but we dream of a better time when the State will undertake the rôle of parents towards those poor children in whose home there is no light and no bread. Then, surely, there will not be so many degenerate children as there are to-day.

But if I wished to sum up all that lies in my heart about the bringing up of children, I would say,

"*Give your children inward freedom!* Do not bend their wills unnecessarily, and avoid arousing their defiance. Teach them the love of the good and the beautiful. Teach them, not through edifying conversations, nor by pious tracts, nor through fear of your anger or the punishment of God, nor through moral stories. But influence them by your example! Be noble and good, loving and gentle (yet in moderation), be strong and unyielding when the time demands it.

Find out the direction in which lie the chief capabilities of the child who, like a sunflower, turns the whole of his interest towards his future sun. Encourage his interests; do not torment him with your ambitions and your plans. Provide him with the work that will be to him a joy and a recreation. *Then your children will not have to walk in the paths along which misdirected souls, lost, wander when there is no light to show them the way in the darkness.*

CHAPTER XVI

EXCITEMENTS

There are truths which one accepts, in the same unquestioning manner as one takes paper money, because they appear to have the same value as truth. One day it occurrs to some one to examine carefully the real value of the truth, and the supposed truth vanishes and becomes nothing but a well-masked lie. It is similar in the case of counterfeit money, which has a value only so long as its fictitiousness is not discovered. The treasured note then becomes a worthless piece of paper. Indeed every truth is like a bond entirely dependent for its value upon the credit it inspires. The day will come when proud Truth will be dethroned and its place as ruler taken by its enemy, which up to that had been called " Untruth."

One such doubtful truth is the widely spread opinion, that " excitements " are harmful. When there is a discussion among ordinary people about any form of nervous complaint, the first question asked will be whether or not the patient has too much excitement in business or in his domestic circle. Most of a doctor's patients complain to him, that they have had too many excitements, and ask if those are harmful to them? And if it would not be better for them to take it quietly for a time. They envy people who live a quiet life. As, however, there is no business without some excitement, or any family in which life flows on quietly and without change, like a tranquil, steady stream—such envy is ridiculous, and arises from ignorance of the facts of real life.

But as the water of a stream rises and falls, so life is a constant up and down of excitement and worry, and he who does not experience these ups and downs in life, seek for excitements. As a beautiful folk-song, mentioned before, aptly says:

We love to gather pain and care;
We seek for thorns and find them e'er.

No! Excitement does not produce illness. On the contrary, excitements tend to keep one young and in good health. Of course, as in everything else in life, too much may be harmful. But if I were asked which is the more harmful, a peaceful life without any excitement, or an existence full of excitement, I should not hesitate a second before deciding for the latter, as the more healthy. For excitements are not only excitements, but are also incitements. And how poor is the life without the stimulation of incitement. "Nothing is harder to bear than a succession of happy days," runs an old saying, which I still regard as true. A beauty which remains always the same ceases to be beautiful. Beauty is never stationary, but always changing. The fascination of ugliness is only the result of a satiety of beauty. Our life is built up of contradictions. Where there is no light, there can be no shadows, and vice versa; so the charm of peaceful days can only be appreciated by contrast with stormy ones. We need excitement in order that a rest may be a real rest.

This truth dawned on me once, when I became acquainted with a lady who complained of all kinds of nervous afflictions and believed herself in consequence to be unhappy. She was one of those women to whom the short-sighted would say: "What's the matter with you? You have all that heart can desire! You have a good husband who worships you, charming children, a beautiful house, dresses, in short, everything. So what is lacking?"

This lady in fact led the most peaceful life. Her husband, a high official, left his office every day at three o'clock in the afternoon, and returned to his house, having no other interests than his wife and children. (The recognized ideal of all women with very busy husbands.) They would go for a walk, play music, or, if the weather were bad, would read fine books. The husband adored his wife and gave her every attention. What did she lack to complete her happiness? In spite of all, there were times when this woman felt unhappy. At these times she became depressed and monosyllabic, complained of various bodily ills for which no organic foundation could be discovered, and showed those subtle indications of weariness of life which are usually hidden behind slight feelings of anxiety.

Once, in a quiet hour, such as the stormy stress of the day so rarely affords, she opened her heart to me. The monotony of her life, with one day exactly like another, sometimes appeared to her unbearable. However outrageous it may sound, even the illnesses of her children came as a change to her; and I know well enough how tenderly she loved her children. Sometimes the "mad" thought came into her head, "If only he were not such a model husband! If only there would come a change in this eternal sameness." All the woes of a woman whose circumstances were only too happy, and who had never experienced misfortune, were revealed to me. It reminded me of Tannhäuser's cry: "Wenn so ein Gott geniessen kann, ich bin dem Wechsel untertan." (Although a god may be able to continue thus to enjoy, I must have a change.) Or "Aus Freuden sehn, ich mich nach Schmerzen!" (In joy I turn longingly to sorrow.)

Poor woman! Many will smile at this expression of sympathy, and think one might be able to put up with the misfortune of Fortune! But there is really only one kind of unhappiness! To give an example, the cancellation of a barber's visit to a rich man upsets the latter just as much as the lack of sufficient money to pay his rent affects a poor man. One appreciates only the contrasts in life. Therefore the woman was really to be pitied. Her heart cried out for an experience. She longed for excitement. She wanted to burn, to blaze up, and rebelled against a life in which she could only smoulder away. What an oppressive, insupportable contrast to her childhood, when she used to let her fancy roam free in the magic land of unlimited possibilities. There she could experience thousands of adventures. Princes sought her hand, and she refused them all because she loved a poor knight. Triumphantly she resisted temptation when her virtue was in danger. She defended herself against enemies and delighted in her friends. On lonely moonlight nights she heard the post horn, and with Eichendorf, " spread the wings of her soul and flew over the land." Before her stretched the wide, unknown, alluring life. What would it bring? Numberless possibilities floated before her vision and an endless procession of ever-changing figures passed before her. And then, what had real life given to her? One single beautiful reality—but only one. Oh! How she longed for a second.

Those who do not understand this woman will not realize that men and women become unfaithful simply to experience something exciting. Many openly confess, when a fleeting episode of their life has brought them into touch with sin and care, " at least I have lived."

A cry for real life, for burning hours full of excitement, for the straining tension of nerves, resounds through the peace of quiet, homely households where the endless hours crawl like bloodless spectres through the silent rooms. What do men seek but excitement, when reading exciting novels, and detective stories in newspapers. How they crowd into the theatres, in order to be able to live, in the play, a life which in their own circumstances is denied them. The most popular pieces, and those which attract the greatest number, are the exciting plays, full of life—in which the nerves are always in a state of tension. And it is the same with the cinemas, which now have to satisfy the craving of the people for excitement—only those scenes "draw" which are the most exciting—where one sees people in imminent danger of their lives, every moment of the utmost importance for their safety. The heart almost ceases to beat in suspense for the appearance of the rescuer. The wild chase rages over the prairies; deserters escape the bullets of their pursuers by a hairbreadth; heroic maidens rescue the children and the old folk; and at last the tension is released, and all ends up happily in a joyous scene. Thus sufficient excitement to fill a whole lifetime is compressed into one hour. Condensed extracts from life, creating false emotion!

However could such a false doctrine have been spread abroad, as that such an urgent need of people could be harmful, and produce neurosis. How often the doctor has the opportunity of convincing himself of the opposite! It has already been emphasized by past observers of life, how stupidly and excitedly nervous people behave about trifling incidents, whilst in face of great events they behave surprisingly well. Persons who in the ordinary way are incapable of making an independent decision, and who have to ask the opinion of three people before buying a new hat—when suddenly confronted with a difficult task, develop an energy and vigour which astonishes none more than themselves. We would hardly guess how many things, under certain circumstances, serve a curative purpose. A Frenchman, a retired jeweller, named Tavernier, who enjoyed quite a reputation as a traveller, suffered greatly from gout. In the year 1827, when he was in Egypt, he quarrelled with an Aga, with the consequence that the enraged Turk caused him to be bastinadoed without further ceremony. This painful and somewhat unpleasant experience cured Tavernier permanently of his gout. Some may believe that it was the somewhat energetic massage of the soles of the feet which brought about this wonderful cure. (Inventive minds may introduce a new "cure" by the "knock and lash method!")

As a matter of fact, it was already known to the earlier doctors that great excitement is an excellent cure for gout. Perhaps an attack of gout is best met by an outbreak of rage, and this method was in earlier times actually put into practice, and sufferers from gout used to swear and rage when the attack came, and thereby experienced great relief. But artificial excitement is only a surrogate of little value, compared with the great excitement which comes from external sources and which it cannot replace.

A very instructive case of a great excitement acting as a remedy is related in the famous work by the well-known French scientists Raymond and Janet, entitled, *Fragments des leçons cliniques du mardi.* It deals with a thirty-seven-year-old lady who suffered from severe attacks of anxiety and depression. She had her first attack on the occasion of her marriage, when she was twenty years of age. It was very critical and lasted for six months. Similar attacks occurred from time to time. She complained of all sorts of pains in the stomach which prevented her from eating, and so caused her to lose flesh. Pains in the head, pains in the back, and pains in every joint completed the picture of ill-health. In adddition to all this there was an alarming absence of will and loss of will power. When she was in bed, it required a great effort of will for her to get up. If she got up, it was just as difficult for her to lie down again. She hesitated and wavered over the most trifling questions. "It seems as if I am quite unable to perform the smallest task," she said; "I cannot make up my mind to do it. If at last I make the decision, then I find it goes quite easily."

This unsatisfactory state of things lasted for two

years, until a cure was effected in a remarkable way by a great excitement. The lady, herself the mother of two children, was visiting a niece who was about to become a mother, when the latter suddenly began to complain of pain. No one was at hand, and the child did not wait for the services of the midwife, but took it upon himself to make his entry into the world. Our patient, owing to the rapidity of the event, was obliged to take over the rôle of midwife. The self-control she had to exert, the excitement, and perhaps also the astonishment she felt at being able to help to bring a healthy boy into the world, brought about in her a tremendous change; she felt as if something in her head had stirred, and she at once declared herself cured. The next day she called in order to relate her adventure and her entire recovery, which has now been complete during the last two years. It is a pity that this method of therapy cannot be applied to every case of neurasthenia. Thus ends the report of the interesting case of the above-mentioned authors.

What can we learn from this remarkable case? That many people suffer from weakness of will, because life has never given them the opportunity to prove their capabilities and to do some work, to have means to turn to account all their energies, to develop all their capabilities, to work and to struggle. What does it matter whether one excites oneself more or less? What we want to know is for what purpose one excites oneself. If it is for a great idea, a great work, a great aim, then certainly those excitements will not be harmful. If, however, we dissipate our psychic energy in small everyday affairs, if we fight with dwarfs instead of with giants and gods, if our affects stir only the surface of a swamp instead of filling the sails of a hurrying ship, then we are rebellious and full of defiance at a fate which compels us to be passive when we wanted to be creative, to vegetate and to dream when we wished to blossom and to grow.

Therefore one should look for plenty of opportunities for excitement for oneself. Those who have cultivated a keen taste for art and nature have always a sufficiency of excitement, because they always have scope for glowing enthusiasm. Their blood will flow more quickly through their veins, and the dross of bodily weakness will be melted in the fire of their psychic emotions; in this I see the explanation of the otherwise inexplicable fact, that artists, who live in a world of constant excitement, so long preserve their youth; and that learned men, who pass their time between dusty books and vaporous laboratories, retain their virility so long, and continue, untiring, their work. Life is a magic torch like Aladin's wonderful lamp; the more vigorously and strongly it burns, the longer it will keep alight. He who throws himself into life the most whole-heartedly, lives the longest. From the flame of one's own psyche grows power; and from the ashes of passion, rises ever anew—like the Phœnix, with undamaged wings—joy in enjoyment and in creative work.

CHAPTER XVII

THE KING'S SPECTACLES

A LETTER to one and to many.

You wish to know what I think of your plan? You wish to go into the charmingly situated sanatorium in N. and in the three weeks you are spending there you want to go in for a little psycho-analysis. That means you want to see your innermost soul in order to judge other people's souls more rightly and value them better.

Hebbel says that man, Basilisk-like, dies when he sees his innermost soul. Have you thought this well over? Psycho-analysis may be compared with a serious operation. One does not undergo laparotomy from sheer pleasure, or to find out what the appendix looks like. Only under necessity do we submit ourselves to the knife of the surgeon. It is unwise frivolously or from curiosity to desire to unveil the image at Sais. I will reply to this inquiry of yours (which is to-day a burning question) in more detail.

Do not be surprised if I digress somewhat, I have just a free hour and the theme needs a very thorough discussion.

Where shall I start? . . . I find it difficult to make a beginning. Well, once upon a time then—— Why not relate a fairy-tale when one wishes to talk about cruel reality? Fairy-tales are truth in the guise of fiction. At present, humanity is so constituted that it can always swallow lies more easily than truth, and probably this will always be the case. Therefore we will begin our scientific investigation under the guise of a fairy-tale. But there are also scientific fairy-tales, which are lies in the garb of truth. What is now left of the confused tangle of so-called Science of a hundred years back? Only a more or less pretty fairy-tale! On the other hand a great many miraculous tales have become reality, such as wireless telegraphy, flying, the telescope, the Röntgen rays. So we have good reason for beginning as though we were telling a real fairy-tale. Once upon a time there was a short-sighted king, who desired to know, to see, to hear, to feel, and to understand all things, in order that he might make every one happy. He believed that his senses were too poor and too dull for a king so extraordinary as himself, and with such unusual intentions;

so he begged and implored all the good spirits to endow him with the finest senses possible. He worried most of all about his big, ugly spectacles. He became so troubled and so unhappy over his own supposed short-comings that the fairies agreed to grant him for one day the gift of the most delicate senses. They hoped by doing this to cure him and to make him happy once more. For one day he should need no spectacles, and he should have the keen eye of the eagle, the hearing of the wild cat, the sense of smell of a bloodhound, the sense of touch of the bat, and the palate of the most fastidious cook in the royal palace.

Was there a happier man than our king now? He could hardly wait till the next day in order to enjoy and make use of his fine senses. It had been decreed that the magic should begin to work at eight o'clock in the morning. In greatest excitement the king kept looking at his watch when he was alone in his bedroom. The spectacles lay safely inside their case. Suddenly a very unpleasant odour assailed his sensitive nose. He noticed what he had never noticed before, that his bedroom was not yet aired. He felt as though he would suffocate, so oppressive was the stale atmosphere around him. He rang for his valet, and the piercing sound hurt his ears. The servant entered with heavy tread, in spite of his efforts to creep gently in his velvet slippers. But, oh! how dirty he seemed to the astonished king. His Majesty noticed that he had washed but cursorily, and that he brought with him the unpleasant smell which is generally attached to the stable. "Were you away from the Palace last night?" he inquired of the valet, whose duty it was to sleep in the king's ante-chamber, and to be at his beck and call during the night. The servant trembled like an aspen-leaf, for he had taken French-leave, and had left his post; a transgression for which he would be severely punished. He made use of the first lie which occurred to him. He had, he said, a sweetheart who was one of the stable-maids, and he had gone out to visit her for a few hasty moments. The king read in his face that this was not the truth. He also observed—what is always very unpleasant to experience—the half-concealed envy, the secret defiance, the suppressed rebellion, the growing impulse for revenge, characteristic of the servile class. He was deeply astonished and decided to dismiss his servant at once. At the king's angry gesture of dismissal the man silently went away, after opening the window. Outside the Palace gate stood two guards, whispering quietly to each other. When they saw the king without his spectacles they paid no heed to him. The king could see quite clearly their malicious looks and could hear their words. . . . " The stupid king, he believes that his beloved, beautiful mistress is faithful to him. Last night I myself saw the yellow-haired chamberlain creeping to her room." To which the other replied: " How should she be content with our old man here. If I were a lovely courtesan, I should know how to find a better companion than this old short-sighted greybeard. . . ." The king hardly dared to trust his own ears. What! was it in such a disrespectful manner his own guards spoke of him? these his favourites, in whom he confided and whom he spoilt with presents and kindness? But worse was to follow. The ministers came to pay their respects. The king saw through their outward appearance into their hearts and from small signs realized their falseness and craftiness. And wherever he found loyalty and love, there also was deceit and hatred. At last, alone in his own room, he made his supplication: Almighty God, grant me to see but one single-minded, faithful human being. Grant that I may see some hearts which beat in that true devotion to myself of which I have been assured so often.

He did not venture to leave his room again that day. He cursed his acute senses, which had opened up to him the secret meaning of the Universe, and he longed for his former condition and his sheltering spectacles. He counted the minutes, but time seemed to stand still. It crawled slowly, like a snail over a dry hillock. Then he summoned his favourite court physician; and observed how the latter trembled for his life before him.

He had no desire to inquire further, as to whether that might be from love, or from anxiety for the precious life of the king with which he had been entrusted. He asked for a sleeping-draught and slept until late next morning. He could not succeed, as he would have wished, in making himself believe that yesterday's experience was nothing but a bad dream. His trust in Humanity was shaken, and he no longer wished to rule. He saw himself surrounded by so much envy, mistrust, hatred, danger, and defiance, and he realized that in benefiting one, he was injuring another, and that he sowed at the same time love and hatred, gratitude and ingratitude.

Here ends our fairy-tale. We need not draw a moral lesson from it, but let us state this truth (turning again to reality), that we are all blind to the true inner aspect of things, and that every one sees even the external phenomena of the Universe through the disturbing medium of his own emotions. Wherever the affect plays a part, there all Logic is at an end. People are surprised that others act so irrationally in allowing themselves to be deceived, and in believing so readily in tales which any one else can easily see through. But in reality we are all like players in a game of chess. The onlooker always perceives the best moves, he foresees danger, and he guesses the plans of the opponent. The player himself may easily be blinded by his own affect.

The distorting effect of one's affects shape the world according to one's own desires. The lover sees only the merits of his beloved: the antagonist sees only the faults and weaknesses of his enemy: the man who serves sees ever before his eyes the coveted object which obliterates everything else. Through our affects we become short-sighted, and therefore all the small conflicts of life acquire for us an over-emphasized significance. Women especially, whose disposition is much more primitive than that of men, yield more easily to their emotions and limit their horizon by all sorts of affects, till finally they cannot see any further than their own limited domain; namely, their housekeeping, their children, and their servants; and all conflicts are staged in this narrow sphere. Since human beings cannot live without conflict, and since fighting and playing are essential elements in life, they fight with their dearest surroundings over the trifles of everyday life, and play tragic rôles for the most trivial motives.

When people fall ill, the everyday routine seems to stand still for a while, their horizon broadens and they see, beyond their limited sphere of work and cares, deeper into the Universe, and grasp the meaning of life. For a moment they lay aside their spectacles and enjoy the wide limitless perspective. Then they make fine praiseworthy resolutions; they will no longer be foolish, nor give themselves up to trivial cares; they feel that one should enjoy life and make good use of time, and rise above the ridiculous pin-pricks of fate.

The first days and weeks after recovery are truly wonderful; one wants to take deep draughts of the glowing cup of life; one yearns to be good, to show kindness, to seize in one grasp all the delights of this world; to forgive, to understand, to get true enlightenment, to enjoy and to let others enjoy. Alas! how swiftly it disappears, this beautiful intoxication and this free enlightenment. We put the old spectacles on again, at first grumblingly; then we harness ourselves willingly once more to the well-known yoke, and become yet again the old short-sighted bamboozled beast of burden.

If even the normal man is unable to see the world with unaided eyes, (and it is certainly a very wise provision of nature that he does not do so, for otherwise he would fare as our poor short-sighted king!) the neurotic can only be understood if we imagine him as a man who is wearing incorrect and unsuitable spectacles. All the near things appear to him to be far away, as though he were looking through the wrong end of a pair of opera-glasses. Distant things seem to be within his reach; time with him is not according to that shown by his watch, but Past and Future are merged into one, and the Present has lost all value to him.

His spectacles have distorted his vision; but, strangely enough, he has so accustomed himself to his faulty glasses that he cannot adapt himself to any others.

Sportsmen have observed that when newly wearing glasses, which may be perfectly adapted to their faulty eyesight, they are not able to shoot with accuracy. They have become accustomed to the incorrect focus of their eyes. The same occurs in the case of the Neurotic, and it is this which makes the cure of these people so difficult—often almost impossible. We could give many examples to illustrate this. For instance there is the type of the younger brother, who, in his childhood, had to observe with envy how his brother took advantage of the two years by which he was the elder. He himself always had to obey, whereas the elder brother was allowed to do things which, to him, were forbidden. He was always left in the background, while the other one was praised and spoilt.

Such people then, through their whole life, continue to wear these spectacles of childhood. They always see themselves neglected, there is always some one else who deprives them of success, who marries the prettiest girl under their noses, and carries out his own secret plans; always there is somebody who is standing in their light. In their outlook on the world they see only the person just in front, who is invariably a step in advance of them. We must rob such a person of his spectacles, and get him accustomed to seeing the world as it is, and not as he imagines it to be.

There are others who have had a very strict father, who ostensibly has shown them too little love. These again, see this father reflected in their life, and cannot rid themselves of the "Father-complex."

They are always ready to complain of insufficient

recognition by their superiors, but seek ever to place themselves in the same position over and over again. (Nietzsche's law of recurrence.) I know a doctor who came into conflict with the chief and all the assistants in every clinic, and had to leave after a short time.

Only by correcting the faulty spectacles through which he saw his superiors was he enabled to remain in one place, and to specialize in one branch of science.

Another wears the spectacles of work-shyness, and rests upon the hope that he will come into an inheritance. He comes of a wealthy family, and has rich relatives from whom he will some day inherit. Already when at school, he heard that he was fortunate in that he need not exert himself so much as the others, as he could expect as much money as he could want, in addition to having a rich aunt and so on.

Naturally the boy stopped learning, and feigned sickness for this purpose. He stood between different relatives whom he was obliged continually to see, and to enter into their different idiosyncrasies. (Or so he was told at home.) One aunt was particularly religious, and there he had to pretend piety. Another one was liberal minded; and there he must not talk of religion. A third vacillated between different opinions.

So he became a man without a purpose, but with the one secret hope of becoming an heir. He gave a wide berth to work, because it would make him fit to earn his living, and that would free his relations from the obligation to think of his future before their death.

He spoilt his life because he did not want to do without his spectacles, which conjured before his vision a world without work, as the highest aim. This man also must remove his spectacles in order to be able to enjoy life.

What a diversity of spectacles there are which these people wear, and how difficult this makes it to distinguish between normal and abnormal people. I will mention only the spectacles of nationality, which magnify the qualities of our own nation and minimize those of foreigners; the spectacles of race, the spectacles of religion, the spectacles of scientific conviction, the spectacles of mysogony, and the spectacles of philanthropy.

These be-spectacled people always see a false aspect of the world, because the true aspect would be unbearable to them.

We need illusions for life. The value of reality is generally placed too low by people. A brilliantly painted Hope is still always more highly valued than a Reality with a fair chance of enjoyment. We require deceptions, because life itself—as it really is—is of no value to us.

Is the Psalmist right when he holds that pain and toil are the most precious jewels of life? And shall we keep before our eyes the idea that everything, —honour, fame, gain, enjoyment—is only a fleeting illusion to disguise from us the emptiness and uselessness of our existence? Are we to learn, as the wise Seneca asserts, that there is no pure love, no true and disinterested friendship, that in the ancient thickets of the soul slumber the menacing primaeval animal instincts, that man is to man as the wild beast? *Homo homine lupus!*

No! I extol the good, useful spectacles which produce before us a non-existent world. Non-existent, but some day to be. The man of to-day is a transition stage of the future man. We behave as if we were noble men, and, lo! we grow to our part. We love the Good for the sake of goodness; we see no evil and evil ceases to exist for us. And we can remove our spectacles and learn that the primaeval instincts are beasts of prey, whose fangs have lost their edge; that neurosis is a serpent, whose poison is no longer effective.

And what about the fairy-tale with which I began this chapter? Yes!—the end is still to come. The king called his wise men and asked them to cure him and to explain to him the badness of this world. An old seer was found who was able to satisfy the king's desires. He said: "Mighty King, clearly have you seen the evil, but you have not marked that these people have only done what was right. They are loyal to you to the death. They allow themselves to be killed for you; they acclaim you when you pass in your sedan. That is to say they have conquered the evil in themselves. They have striven with themselves, they still strive and retain the victory. What more can you want? Do you want to change man's nature and to tear the evil out of his breast? It is just their virtue and privilege that they actually do only the good. That you cannot bear the sight of Truth proves how wise kind Fate was in inflicting short-sightedness upon you and giving you spectacles. Forget that which you have seen, and wear your spectacles patiently and with dignity."

The king pondered long, and found that the wise man was right as most wise men are. He made his peace with himself, with his spectacles, and with those around him, and "lived." . . . .

Here the fairy-tale stops again. I have told it to those people who are at cross-purposes with themselves and with the world; who have had a glimpse of their own souls and have shrunk from the Truth. The king is oneself, and the servants are wishes. The rebellions are one's impulses, the guards are inhibitions. The gift of the sharpened senses is a bad conscience, this present-day disease of good people—because all neurotics suffer from their goodness. It shows our faults magnified and exaggerated, and our virtues minimized out of recognition. Fearfully, we take up again our spectacles, and so correct the unpleasant Truth by new illusions. Whoever has the courage to take off his spectacles must also take into consideration the words of the wise man, to own up to his weaknesses, and to welcome the overcoming of these as a victory and triumph. Thus every one who seeks and understands becomes the door-keeper of a new world; a world with no spectacles.

Whether that is ever possible or not, I cannot decide. I have only related a fairy-tale—a scientific fairy-tale having a real background lit up by the glowing dawn of a new day.

* * * * * * * *

I wanted to tell you that. Now you can form your own opinion from the fairy-tale and from the essay. But I think that you would rather keep to your old thick spectacles, and that you will regard "a little Psycho-analysis" as a necessity for the sufferer, but a danger for the healthy. Keep your beloved old thick spectacles then! Praise your shortsightedness! But let me tell you two lines from Hugo von Hofmannsthal: "I shudder, I do not want to stand before the mirror—in which I should see my *entire* self."

CHAPTER XVIII

HOLIDAYS

When I leave home on a Sunday afternoon to plunge into the whirl of the festive crowd, my glance involuntarily falls on a clean, widely-opened window of the grey house opposite. At this window sits an elderly gentleman, gazing contentedly through his gold spectacles on the crowded street below. Ah, I thought to myself at first, here is one who no doubt loves to go out in the evening, when the first shadows are stealing over the quiet streets. Soon I was to know better. At any hour of a holiday I would find this tranquil old gentleman at his post, and he always looked down upon us so complacently, as if he were judging human affairs from a higher range of experience. An eccentric, I decided, losing himself in his reveries, and whose quiet room contains his whole world. Or was he perhaps an invalid? No, that could not be, for his healthy, well-nourished appearance was against such an idea. Besides, on week-days I was often able to admire his tall, distinguished figure and his fine, elastic gait.

Once as I returned home from the Prater,* dusty, tired, and worn out, the real explanation of my kindly neighbour dawned on me. He was doubtless a philosopher, one of the few wise men who do not allow themselves to be ruled by conventions, but who go their own way.

He has discovered the secret of our so-called festive joys. He knows quite well that we are vaguely deceiving ourselves, through the power of our imaginaton, into believing that we have been enjoying ourselves, whereas in truth we have enjoyed none of those sensations of pleasure that we were bent on pursuing. Quietly he sits at his post, smoking his pipe, glancing now and then at his paper which tells him of war, conflagration and murder, of the strivings and desires of humanity, of wishes attained and buried. With a quiet superiority he looks down upon us slaves of Sunday, who for an idea are robbing ourselves of a real joy, an actual need—rest, in order to pursue an imaginary one. I understand the meaning now of his subtle smile,

* A park in Vienna.

which used to follow me when I went and when I returned. On one occasion I tried following his example, took a choice cigar and a good book and sat down at my window. What an agreeable little panorama I had before me, free of charge! What a double side all and everything has in this world!

There they passed before me, the holiday-slaves: dressed up servant-girls, wasting their slender wages on fine dresses, so as to ape "ladies of high rank" for a few miserable hours; the anxious mother with her overdressed daughters, seeking with difficulty to hide their poverty behind showy garments; the tired labourer, his little child on his arm, his pipe in his mouth, followed by his sullen-looking, prematurely aged wife, who is mentally calculating the cost of the Sunday outing, and anticipating gloomy week-days, while possessed by the one hope that things might go off this time without the usual bout of drunkenness; the careless student, a flower in his buttonhole, eager for conquests and on the point of committing some great folly; soldiers from the country on the quest for love and a hot supper; thousands of parents with children of all ages, trying to give them some pleasurable excitement, and thus to enable them to warm their own disappointed, cold hearts at the fire of youth . . . and countless other figures, a strange procession, a pilgrimage into the longed-for land of Sunday-joys.

In thought I followed them to their destinations; I saw them, heated and excited by passions, crowding into stuffy, smoke-filled rooms. I saw them wandering in dusty, overcrowded gardens, jostling and ogling each other, as if to see faces were one of the greatest joys in the world. I saw them fighting to buy a morsel of food at a high price, saw them swallow it greedily, while blaring music scarcely drowned the hubbub of voices. Now I began to realize the full absurdity of many things. The bitter struggle for a seat in the Underground electric, the tram or motor-bus, the breathless rushing through the beauties of Nature, watch in hand, and worried by perpetual anxiety lest they should miss the last train which would carry them, poor slaves, back to the treadmill of daily life.

Truly—the whole restlessness of our time is shown by the way in which we kill our holidays. Should they not be days of rest for soul and body? Should we not quietly think of past times, weigh one experience against another, and prepare ourselves for the strife of the coming days? What does our rest really amount to? Noise, dust, excitement, danger, overfatigue, jaded nerves. How many, through such amusements, may have acquired the germs of disease, while their work has never done them any harm! Are these amusements really a pleasure? Surely not! This kind of amusement resembles work as one egg resembles another.

Suddenly, I remembered an experience of my own happy student days. Indeed, I was a happy student in the true sense of the word, who imbibed freely of all the joys that a big town could offer in the way of Science, Art, Nature, Sport and social gatherings, but who never sacrificed an hour's sleep, except for a high stake, and who never arranged his holiday according to the calendar. I chose mine according to my mood. Now for my experience.

A hot day in June. I close my book, finding it impossible to study. Four o'clock in the afternoon. I feel an immense craving for air, for green trees, for shady meadows in the twilight. In an instant I am out in the street, striding rapidly along. I go on foot as far as the suburbs, because from there onward the bus fare is considerably cheaper. Then up to the lofty seat behind and overlooking the driver. Slowly the clumsy vehicle takes me to Neuwaldegg. At last I am in the forest! How still and peaceful it all is, in the eternal festival of Nature. How different the whole aspect of things from that of a week-day.

Flowers bloom close to the edge of the path as if they knew that no cruel hand could now pluck them senselessly, and out of a brutal delight in plunder, only to throw them away again carelessly; birds warble from the low-hanging branches their exquisite work-a-day songs, which no Sunday visitor can ever hear. No human being in sight! No tourist with decorated hat, tweed suit and gaudy tie, with the absurdly unsuitable and pretentious alpenstock, the crammed rucksack and heavily nailed mountain boots. To left and right of the path, greasy scraps of paper, empty bottles, initials cut into the trees, testify that a host of holiday-makers have been behaving like Vandals.

On and on I go. A startled hare darts across my path, doubtless not a little surprised at my unexpected intrusion. Where is chance leading me? I come to a quiet, friendly inn, where a solitary guest is seated at a neatly laid table. With what attention I am received and served! The host enters into a confidential chat with me and asks me in a friendly way where I am going, and if I am satisfied with the food and drink. He also remarks that it is very quiet here on week-days, but that if I would come on a Sunday I should hear a tip-top "Viennese Quartet." I thank him kindly, but observe that I much prefer the symphony in the green trees, which remark so charms my solitary neighbour that he seats himself at my table, just as in Uhland's "Krug zum Grünen Kranze." He invites me to drive home with him. He is a coachman and has just driven out a gentleman and his lady. He would willingly give me a seat beside him on the box. I thank him politely for his friendly offer, but tell him that I am walking farther.

Here is an inscription on a tablet which I had not noticed before. "Here Adalbert Stifter wrote his 'Field Flowers' . . ."

Adalbert Stifter—poet of rest and of joy in Nature. Thrice blessed be thou, quiet forest-inn!

I plunged deeper into the forest. By chance I took the path towards Hütteldorf. It grew darker. The sun had gone down behind the tall trees and a strange twilight flooded the clear air. Was it a fairy-tale, or was it the play of my excited senses? In the midst of this green solitude there sat a stone knight, mourning. He was guarding a tomb in the quiet loneliness of the forest. I could hardly make out the inscription. The grave of Laudon. I was filled with a chill sense of the perishableness of all things. Never shall I forget that half-hour spent alone in the forest before the tombstone, caressed by the soft scents of evening, surrounded by ghostly figures from centuries long past. Had Romance then not yet died out? Had the enthusiastic poems of Eichendorff become reality?

The twilight deepened, and I had to hurry if I did not wish to be overtaken by the night. Now appeared the first lights of Hütteldorf, where I knew of good friends whom I wanted to surprise with my late visit. Through the open window of the villa, I could see them sitting round a table enjoying themselves. Now out with my latest favourite song (I had a new one every month!):

"When we roam through the streets . . . "

resounded through the quiet night. What a surprise for them and how pleasantly passed the hours—until the last train, which took me safely back to the place where I had mounted the coach.

When I compare this and similar experiences with my present holiday pleasures, I am driven to the conclusion that all the misery of the world comes from coercion. Because our Sunday is fixed by calendar, we have to screw ourselves up to the Sunday-mood. We talk a lot about our freedom, are proud of all our acquired "liberties," and yet we overlook the fact that we are miserable slaves: slaves to our circumstances, slaves to our feelings and slaves to our surroundings. This freedom laid down by law—the Sunday of the wage-slaves, is in reality only another form of slavery. The higher the rights of the *masses* become, the smaller grows the right of the *individual.* Every new advance, every new discovery, every new machine, breaks away another stone from the noble edifice of personal freedom, and turns us into machines which work, or cease work, at the will of the factory owner. If my remarks have been carefully followed, it will be seen that neurosis signifies the struggle between the individual and the demands of Society. It is the rebellion of the helot, the protest of the weak against tyranny, the obstinacy of the feeble. It is the clenching of the fist in the pocket, when the desire is to raise it against every authority. We have seen that the neurotic may be either inwardly pious and outwardly unbelieving, or outwardly pious and inwardly unbelieving. We have been able to catch a glimpse of mysterious depths, seen through deep fissures of his psyche, and we have described the silent battle which the unfortunate sufferer wages for the sake of one part of his personality, his Beloved Ego. It was, however, necessary constantly to point out that our present order of society suppresses the right of the individual in favour of the right of the masses. In this respect no improvement is to be expected from Socialism, which already saddles the masses with authority similar to that of Church and State, and it was but a natural step that it should also decree festivals, and appropriate May 1st as a holiday for labour. Its power is based on the suppression of personal ambitions in favour of general economic advantages.

The neurotic is more or less of a spiritual anarchist. He looks upon this lack of independence as a personal injury, and rebels against every form of coercion. The reason his reaction fails so miserably lies in the fact that he has not gained inner freedom. He grovels in the dust before the very authority which he despises, sinks on his knees before his foe, and is content to be able to serve the idol of Power he so despised. In short, he is a "half-man."

I cannot end these remarks without pointing out the paths we must take to regain our health. By health I mean joy in life, and nothing but that.

We must all be prepared to fight for our lost freedom. The strongest motive power in man is his craving for freedom and independence. Thirst for domination and the will to power are only other forms of this impulse towards freedom. He who can command others need expect no commands from them.

He who commands all need not let himself be commanded by any one. But because we have entirely lost our inward and outward freedom, our compensatory ideal of freedom is immeasurably intensified. A man suffering from a compulsion neurosis is the slave of his symptoms and a psychic anarchist, vacillating between the will to power and the will to subjection. In the case of the neurotic, both are caricatured and are expressed in grotesque forms either as submissive Masochism or as proud isolation in the modest garb of the eccentric.

It is the task of us psychic physicians to bring about the substitution of real values for false ones.

We must get at the beautiful and the ugly traits in the caricature, separate them, and exhibit the true picture. We must help our patients to fight for that bit of lost freedom which their personality lacks, we must give them so much reality through inward freedom that they can dispense with the idea of a great historic mission.

But we must have the courage ourselves to checkmate everything that subjugates or restrains us, everything that casts us in one mould and turns us into a herd. Away with all social compulsion, away with every convention, every etiquette, every fashion, away with "what people say or do," away with that which we must do and that which we must not do, in short—away with every duty that is not our duty or that is a superfluous duty.

Let us live our life as noble, good and free creatures! Let us not forget that higher than all oonventions an laws stands the iron law of inward necessity. Let us strive to become our own law-givers. Let us learn to renounce, but from free will, not to please society.

And when we have elevated ourselves *above* ourselves to the proud level of a noble-man, then we shall be able to celebrate a festival. For every victory which we have won without compulsion, solely in the light of our own ethics, our own judgement, our own strong resolution, is a victory for humanity. Every good deed performed, not through fear of the punishment of hell or as a miserable bargain for the kind of recompense which rewards good deeds with eternal bliss, is a step towards the splendid temple of the man-of-the-future.

I believe in this future, I believe in the victory of good, I believe in man. Just because I have come to recognize how deep his primal instincts reach down into the savage, the animal, the uncontrolled, boundless and terrible—just because of this fact I see a better future. I realize that we are all the victims of inordinate and unbridled desires, which are striving to come to the surface. I realize that our sufferings, our fears, our doubts, are forces though which this upward striving expresses itself. I feel that we are fighting for the rights of personality, for liberties for which we are not yet ripe. And the days on which I can feel this, such days are my festivals.

APHORISMS

CERTAIN thoughts lose their significance as soon as they are put into words: such value as they have is due to the momentary emotion.

The simplest definition of psycho-analysis: to recognize oneself in another.

Why does speech relieve us? Why must we have an outlet in speech, and why are we unable to tackle our problems alone? Is not a fundamental educational error responsible for this? The Greeks learnt their philosophy from famous masters. But "Philosophy" really means to ask oneself questions and to answer oneself.

If my thoughts are inconsistent, if to-day I maintain the contrary to that which I believed yesterday, it only proves my courage to give expression to the *universal human*.

"Conviction." That is the pass-word of to-day.

There is only one teacher: Experience.

Genius sees more deeply than the so-called normal man, because it concentrates immense energy on a single point. It therefore sees farther in one particular direction, but, unfortunately, in one only, that is, in its own direction. That is why genius can be so blind to everything which lies outside the line of its vision. Talent can often be more just, and substitute breadth for depth of conception.

Every genius has characteristics which betray his littleness, and thus compensate in smallness for his greatness. One must excuse the weaknesses of the great for the sake of their greatness. To see their greatness only, one must not come near them; they must be enjoyed from a distance, through their works.

Intolerable are those small men in whom a slight touch of genius lends the appearance and behaviour of the great. Their shortcomings are unbearable because the compensating greatness is represented only by a pretence of greatness, by megalomania. They give themselves the airs of genius.

There is also a tyranny of progress and of dogmatism which sails upon the sea of knowledge and displays the flag of exploration. The slightest murmurs of opposition on the part of the crew are condemned as rebellion and punished with scientific oblivion.

The envy of ordinary people is more honest than that of the great. The small know that they envy, and occasionally find it painful. The great rationalize their envy in order not to admit it. The more they deprecate the thing they envy, the greater seems their own secret idol—the beloved Ego.

Preconceptions are the executioners of truth.

Genius is never recognized by its contemporaries. Why? Because greatness can be recognized only after the petty details in the picture are forgotten.

The most serious traumata are those which have never occurred. Every trauma is at any rate an experience. Neurosis is the reaction to that which has never occurred. The neurotic's feeling of guilt always relates to what he *might* have done. It is only a masked form of anticipated pleasure. He behaves as though he really had sinned.

The deepest remorse is just that for which there is no justification. A clever woman once said: "I regret that there is nothing I have to regret."

We are said to live again in our children and in those for whom we care. How utterly false! We only deceive ourselves again into thinking that in this way we shall continue to live. Those who experience much live only for themselves, and therefore they seem to be egoists. But is there a greater egoist than the altruist who exploits another in order to make a fuller life for himself?

Morality protects the weak, but does not limit the strong.

Timid persons are like locomotives in which the fires are kept at a low heat so that the engine may stop quickly when the brakes are applied. They run on half steam.

Reality changes birds of paradise into sparrows. Fantasy transforms sparrows into birds of paradise.

Friendship is the tombstone of love.

Who, knowing the soul of the neurotic, would have the courage to speak of a murderous guilt? A tiny wheel that controls the impulses had momentarily ceased to function.

Some passions are like Swedish matches. They must be rubbed across an inflammative compound before they take fire. Let this example serve for many: men are ignited by men and burnt by women. The most important function of a friend of the family is to lend fire to both.

All my patients, probably in common with all men, betray a desire to acquire an enormous fortune with the least expenditure of effort. There will always be more people who dream of drawing the first prize than the humble minded who accept life's blanks.

Work is said to sweeten life. On the contrary! Work is the bitter pill which makes palatable the cloying sweetness of life.

Work is, and must be, the best remedy for all nervous disorders. But only *our own* work, not *any* work. The secret of success and contentment lies in finding one's own fitting work, and this is much more difficult than is generally believed.

So many voices from the outer world resound in our ears that the voice which speaks within us is drowned.

A great thought is a Siegfried releasing a Brunhilde from a flaming sea of unconscious inhibitions.

Ideals require the remoteness of fantasy. Reality depreciates the over-valued by an over-correction downwards. The highest must occasionally be converted into the lowest.

Should it not be taught that Egoism is a duty? Only when we give expression to all our capabilities do we fulfil our human obligations. But humanity and society seem to be irreconcilable antagonists.

Our calling is a concession to the demands of society. It ought to be that form of activity to which one feels oneself "called." Unfortunately one's calling is generally work in an alien sphere and for alien interests.

Who has the courage to confess that he works only because he must? What excesses are concealed behind our work! In truth one needs a good conscience to be able to refrain from work and to give one's thoughts free scope.

The sick over-estimate the importance of their illness; the healthy under-estimate the value of health. Only those exceptional individuals who hover between illness and health are really capable of a proper valuation. One fact, however, is certain: illness separates, health unites; illness exalts and health abases. The highest achievements do not emanate from the healthy. He who enjoy good health does not create; he lives. The sufferer creates in striving for health.

To some people marriage is a compulsion-neurosis in which fidelity is the "over-valued idea."

Hygiene is the modern religion. The micro-organisms invisible to the eye and discoverable only by the microscope are the power which operates in secret. The deity has been transformed from supernatural greatness into unnatural smallness. Small souls have small gods.

The Christian religion allows of the sublimation of all erotic impulses. It has all the elements: the child, the husband, the wife and the father. It is a compromise between the dogmatic monotheism of the Jews and the polytheism of the Greeks. But as there is only one love, so, notwithstanding all attempts at analysis into three elements, there is only one God.

Statistics is the art of lying with numbers.

Ideals are the subterfuges of commonplace souls.

Sometimes it requires more courage to confess a virtue than a vice.

Depression is virtuous lamentation which weeps that it is not wise.

Sympathy is the cruelty of the weak.

Illness is the stronghold of personality.

A display of pride is like the policy of the big business man, who deals in false values in order to get credit—and who succeeds in most cases. Most people grow into the part they play, if only they play it long enough. The garment becomes a second skin.

Our hate is directed towards our superiors and our contempt towards our inferiors. We save ourselves from feeling envy by depreciating our opponents. Instead of acknowledging that we hate his greatness, we pretend to despise his smallness.

I never recognized any other opponents than those who understood—and envied me. The man who does not understand can never be my real opponent. He speaks a foreign tongue.

A man's true greatness is shown by the manner in which he attacks his adversary. If people only realized how they debased *themselves* when they seek to depreciate another, they would depreciate that other in only one way, viz.: creating new values by their own efforts. The other grows smaller only as we grow larger.

Pedagogues atone for the faults of their education by heaping up a multitude of fresh educational errors, which in their turn create again pedagogues from the crippled souls.

Pedagogy should be the orthopædics of the soul. If only it did not further distort and cripple the "ego"!

No belief can ever die. Our childhood beliefs exert their influence all our lives.

We live only once, but once is mostly not at all.

Truths are cleverly disguised lies.

Chastity is the tombstone whose faded letters announce the charms of a dead vice.

Professors are usually the sworn guardians of truths, and wear the countenance of Hippocrates. Death shines in their faces.

Great movements never emanate from official sources.

Laziness is a disproportion between will and power. What is attained seems trivial in comparison with what one aspires to.

Inventions are a translation of personal problems into social problems. Often enough they are the transposition of a psychic problem into a mechanical one.

Marriage is that relationship in which the slavery of the one is alleviated by the bondage of the other.

Sons caricature the faults of their parents, so that these failings often give rise to virtues. But the contrary may also occur. Hence excellent fathers often have worthless sons.

The ideal is the attainable goal which we do not *wish* to attain. There are wishes before whose fulfilment we recoil, because with their fulfilment they would cease to be wishes. Reality depreciates.

Jealousy may be the reaction to a wish to be relieved of an irksome obligation. The infidelity of the other frees us and absolves *us* from the obligation.

We are born aristocrats, and we have to free ourselves into a democratic outlook on life.

Ascetism is the Harakiri of our immortality.

To live means to expend the "interest" on one's allotted time. But most persons take it to mean to use up their capital, and thus the "interest" gets smaller and smaller.

Spring is the transformation of the temporal into an image of the eternal.

The higher our ideal, so much the deeper may we fall.

Sympathy is the dawn of love. Antipathy its sheet lightning.

Experience is the tombstone of fantasy. The dreamer shuns the fulfilment of his yearnings.

There are students of research who always think themselves robbed of their due, and who never cease quarrelling about priority. Truly the claim for priority in thought is not worth a mess of pottage, for each new thought is the infinitesimal last link of old thought. . . . With equal right each new individual might claim the credit for the whole culture of humanity!

Fellow-men! Remain alone and avoid the stimulus supplied by

the herd. Sheep move in dense flocks. The falcon soars lonely through the skies. . . . Associations of people are the destruction of the individual.

Most persons have over them a tyrant whom they serve gladly and willingly: public opinion. What will people say? But what we fear is only our own inner voice, and in reality people only say what we have already told ourselves.

To gain inner freedom: overcome the past, bear the present, and remain untroubled in face of the future.

Pride is the compensation for some shortcoming, and the mask for dissatisfaction.

Remorse is often only a pretext devised for the purpose of revelling in a pleasurable remembrance.

Feelings are the garments of the soul.

Philosophy searches out the problems which are inherent in our daily life. It may prove a great danger to every science because it distorts plain facts with complicated questions.

The dullest minds feel themselves called upon to become the illuminators and torch-bearers of their times.

In the darkness even a small light illumines.

The rich do not fear thefts. One who always thinks himself robbed has not much to lose.

Only love gives ungrudgingly.

Illness brings out the true character of a man. This saying of Goethe contains all the wisdom of the world.

Life's greatest charm lies in change. In perpetual sameness we should stagnate. To-day's extravagance is to-morrow's avarice. We must surpass ourselves from day to day.

To be capable of forgiveness is the prerogative of noble souls. May my readers prove to be such!

Let us learn from our experiences, and let us investigate honestly the sources of our successes. Actually every patient has to heal himself. We psycho-therapeutists are a kind of Baedeker with whose aid the patient finds his way through the entanglement of his neurosis. So that at the best we are only guides. Let us not imagine ourselves the creators of a new life.

Whatever evolves was there before. In the psychic life there are no revolutions. Everything develops; and even neurosis does not mean stagnation.

Thoughts! Neither time nor space can limit them; they penetrate doors and gates and walls. And though the goal were as remote as the sun, our longing would find it.

THE END

Definitions of Psycho-Analytical Terms Used.

Agoraphobia: Fear of open space, or of crossing open spaces.

Anaesthesia: Absence of sensation.

Bi-polarity: See page 9.

Complex: A group of emotionally invested ideas partially or entirely repressed.—(ERNEST JONES.)

Dissociation: Splitting of the personality.

Masochism: Gratification, often sexual in character, derived from mental or physical pain, usually inflicted from without. After Sacher-Masoch, who described this perversion.—(PARAPHILY).

Megalomania: Self-delusion of greatness, vast wealth, etc.

Narcissism: Gratification derived from self-admiration; self-love, after Narcissus, the Greek youth in love with his own image reflected in the water.

Rationalisation: Supplying the place of missing (unconscious) links in the chain of reasoning with another (conscious) link. (Frink). The inventing of a reason for an attitude or action the motive of which is not recognized.—(ERNEST JONES).